SAMUEL BECKETT

My Reading

ROSEMARIE BODENHEIMER

SAMUEL
BECKETT

OXFORD
UNIVERSITY PRESS

OXFORD
UNIVERSITY PRESS

Great Clarendon Street, Oxford, OX2 6DP,
United Kingdom

Oxford University Press is a department of the University of Oxford.
It furthers the University's objective of excellence in research, scholarship,
and education by publishing worldwide. Oxford is a registered trade mark of
Oxford University Press in the UK and in certain other countries

First Edition published in 2022

Impression: 1

Published in the United States of America by Oxford University Press
198 Madison Avenue, New York, NY 10016, United States of America

British Library Cataloguing in Publication Data
Data available

Library of Congress Control Number: 2022930709

ISBN 978-0-19-285873-3

DOI: 10.1093/oso/9780192858733.001.0001

Printed and bound in the UK by
Clays Ltd, Elcograf S.p.A.

SERIES INTRODUCTION

This series is built on a simple presupposition: that it helps to have a book recommended and discussed by someone who cares for it. Books are not purely self-sufficient: they need people and they need to get to what is personal within them.

The people we have been seeking as contributors to *My Reading* are readers who are also writers: novelists and poets; literary critics, outside as well as inside universities, but also thinkers from other disciplines—philosophy, psychology, science, theology, and sociology—beside the literary; and, not least of all, intense readers whose first profession is not writing itself but, for example, medicine, or law, or a non-verbal form of art. Of all of them we have asked: what books or authors feel as though they are deeply *yours*, influencing or challenging your life and work, most deserving of rescue and attention, or demanding of feeling and use?

What is it like to love this book? What is it like to have a thought or idea or doubt or memory, not cold and in abstract, but live in the very act of reading? What is it like to feel, long after, that this writer is a vital part of your life? We ask our authors to respond to such bold questions by writing not conventionally but personally—whatever "personal" might mean, whatever form or style it might take, for them as individuals. This does not mean overt confession at the expense of a chosen book or author; but nor should our writers be afraid of making autobiographical connections. What was wanted was whatever made for their own hardest thinking in careful relation to quoted sources and specifics. The work was to go on in the taut and resonant space between these readers and their chosen books. And the interest within that area begins precisely when it is no longer clear how much is coming from the text, and how much is coming from its readers—where that distinction is no longer easily tenable because neither is sacrificed to the other. That would show what reading meant at its most serious and how it might have relation to an individual life.

Out of what we hope will be an ongoing variety of books and readers, *My Reading* offers personal models of what it is like to care about particular authors, to recreate through specific examples imaginative versions of what those authors and works represent, and to show their effect upon a reader's own thinking and development.

ANNE CHENG
PHILIP DAVIS
JACQUELINE NORTON
MARINA WARNER
MICHAEL WOOD

In loving memory
Andrew Von Hendy (1932–2018)

ACKNOWLEDGMENTS

My deepest gratitude is to Philip Davis, who invited me to submit this work for the *My Reading* series and went on, imaginatively and generously, to guide me through its drafts. I also thank my friends Jonathan Strong and Robin Lydenberg, whose keen readings at different stages heartened and helped me. The cover drawing by American artist John Himmelfarb was a great gift, offered by an enthusiastic new reader of Beckett.

I am indebted to The Estate of Samuel Beckett for granting me the rights to publish the many quotations in this book. I thank especially Joanna Marston of Rosica Colin, Ltd., for her dedicated assistance throughout the permissions procedures. I am grateful to Cambridge University Press and the editors of Beckett's correspondence, for permission to quote from the four volumes of *The Letters of Samuel Beckett*, © The Estate of Samuel Beckett. Many thanks as well to Grove/Atlantic Inc. and to Faber & Faber Ltd., for license to quote extensively from Beckett's works. Finally, I would like to thank Jacqueline Norton and Aimee Wright of Oxford University Press for their support and expertise through the publication process.

CONTENTS

INTRODUCTION

My immersion in Samuel Beckett's writing has come to me in later life, as revelation and consolation. During my working years as a professor of English, I occasionally taught Beckett's *Molloy* in courses on the modern novel, and attended performances of *Waiting for Godot* and *Endgame*. I knew that Beckett appealed to me in some way I couldn't get across in class, but the acquaintance went no further. Some years into retirement, after the death of my husband and colleague, Beckett appeared in my mind one morning as if to offer his company. As I began to read, his work called out feelings and tendencies that inhabit my mostly unexpressed consciousness. For all the vast differences between our backgrounds and life experiences, I found that Beckett often moved in my head as a familiar.

Once I began to mention my interest in writing about Beckett, some of my friends were startled. They knew me as someone dedicated to the richly inhabited nineteenth-century worlds created by Victorian novelists. Perhaps they were a bit alarmed, fearing that I had turned to Beckett's bleakness as a depressive reaction to losing the person I loved so dearly, with whom I had shared a life of reading, teaching, and writing. There was some truth in this. Keeping company with Beckett was, at first, a way of continuing my relationship with my late husband. A few sentences from

Molloy had become household words. "Molloy, your region is vast," we might joke after a walk around the block. Old Beckett paperbacks on our shelves had my husband's notes in the margins. Soon, however, it became necessary to get my own copies of those books. As in most writing adventures, the personal grain of sand that got it going was gradually coated with further layers that turned it into something more.

Reading biographies, I discovered that Beckett's mother, like my husband, had been afflicted with a form of parkinsonism that gradually strips away every competence of body and mind. Beckett's letters testify to the distress this raised in him; his novels reveal how the dismantling of a once coherent human personality affected his postwar art. During the years I spent accompanying my husband on the rocky path that stretches from the end of ordinary living to the brink of death, I felt I'd come to know something of the territory inhabited by Beckett's characters. Its pared-down contours remain with me as a truth that the teeming social and ethical worlds of Victorian fiction rarely touch.

The biographies and letters and testimonies of Beckett's friends also sketched a more general portrait that I liked. I was drawn to his doubt, his honesty, his shyness, his silences, the urgency of his need to reimagine his life through writing, his hunger for solitude, and his prickly defense of privacy—all in combination with a gift for kind and generous friendship. As a natural skeptic, I feel right at home in Beckett's narratives, where doubt is a generative force and second thoughts reign. His refusal to countenance theoretical explanations of his work allows me to hear his sentences with ears tuned back in the days before literary reading turned to the abstractions of theory.

Above all, though, I was moved by two aspects of Beckett's art. The first is emotional: his treatments of memory, nostalgia, and grief, and the forms he finds to convey those essential human experiences while avoiding emotional melodrama or sentimentality. The second is playful: Beckett was always finding ways to break the illusion of narrative plausibility and to suggest the inseparability of author, narrator, and character, in defiance of conventional literary manners. I enjoy his performances as a self-conscious narrator. Because they remind me of what on odd process writing is, I experience those literary games as acts of connection and understanding.

The elusive process of artistic creation has always intrigued me. What is the relation between the unresolvable stresses of a particular life and the works that emerge from that writer? Why is it that, for certain people, writing is the solution to the problem of living? I have come to believe that most writing is at least indirectly autobiographical, if only because no one else could have imagined this paragraph or that sentence in the same way. In Beckett's case, the indirection was crucial. He wished to keep a firm barrier between his life and his published work, and managed better than other twentieth-century novelists to avoid the public trappings of authorhood. All the while, he was writing stories about the need for autobiography and the impossibility of writing it truthfully. As a rather private person who has always written about others as a way of understanding and shaping my own flux of thought, I am sympathetic with Beckett's positions.

Although he was endlessly skeptical about language and fictional conventions, writing was Beckett's best company, and his most essential relationship. He sometimes referred to writing as a "pastime," as though it were a hobby. The self-deprecation marks a characteristic reluctance to dignify his achievement, but he chose the word with care: writing passed the time better than anything else he could do. His need for its companionship is expressed throughout his work, never more directly than in the late prose piece called *Company*.

In my experience, the act of writing creates a sense of dialogue between my mind and the sentences that end up on the screen in front of me. The sentences say things I didn't know I thought, prompt me to write the sentence that has to follow, or call out for revision. They are company because they create a persona different from the person I am when I'm otherwise going about my life. How they emerge from my mind remains a mystery that keeps me interested, and gives me a reason to go on. In my seventies, I begin to understand Beckett's realm, where producing narrative is the most meaningful way to ease the passage of life.

As an amateur chamber musician, I also warm to Beckett's love and practice of another art. He was quite a good pianist, devoted to Haydn, Beethoven, and Schubert in particular, though he could also spin out Irish melodies with gusto. Ideally, he wanted his writing to approach the condition of music, as it moves and changes through time, free of denotative meaning. What mattered was rhythm, repetition, variation, shifts of mood, and tempo. Listening to a good recording of a Beckett work is the best way to appreciate the sound-world of his imagination, and it feels a lot like listening to music. The voice moves slowly, taking its time; it rises and falls in volume, moving from agitation to calm, from lyricism to humorous self-mockery. It's possible to imagine musical markings for each new section of narrative: a change of key, a new tempo indication, dynamic markings, or indications of mood.

Earlier novelists created plots with secrets and romances to keep us reading, gave us characters to have emotions about, wrote settings, exotic or recognizable, within which characters moved. Their narratives also move, as if instinctively, from one mode to another: description, dialogue, free indirect discourse, narrative summary, ethical judgment. Though Beckett gradually threw off many of those novelistic moves, he well knew how to pace sentences, change moods, switch from one writing register to another, and get his reader to wonder what would come next. It's impossible to anticipate what might meet you just over the page, or when you might be plunged into a passage of stunning beauty, a comic romp, a burst of emotional honesty, or a passage of compulsive mathematical permutations.

Though essential, writing was also a tortuous struggle for Beckett. His letters to friends constantly express anguished doubt about whether he can begin, whether he can go on, whether he will ever write again, whether what he's written is any good at all. His fear of running out of stories to tell is palpable, and his characters suffer in similar ways. The end words of *The Unnamable*, "I can't go on, I'll go on," appear throughout the work in many variants, meaning both "go on living" and "go on writing."

Reading Beckett can also be a daunting task. It requires that we accept the ground rules of his fictional worlds. For some people this comes readily, while others react with alienation or depression. Why persevere, in this bleak territory deprived of plot or character in the usual sense? How often can we stand to have a glimmer of stable meaning pulled out from under our reading eyes? Half the fun, for me, lies just there, in the drama of doubt and second thought that Beckett's narrators perform in an endless variety of ways. Rarely is something asserted that's not overturned or forgotten afterwards. Language flourishes in the moment of its telling; then it gives way to something else. Beckett gets me to believe that this dynamic is the truth about all the speaking and writing that takes us through our days.

The mordant fictive situations Beckett created are patently unreal—think of ancient parents residing in garbage cans, or a world made of nothing but mud. His characters respond to such conditions with perfectly recognizable sets of worries, speculations, anxieties, fears, and practical adaptations. Conditions are bad; characters become more and more decrepit. Yet they go on dealing with what comes their way, engaging a full repertoire of human emotions. Feelings flash out from a corner turned between sentences, from a hilarious imitation of the way our minds worry to ourselves, or from Beckett's powerful metaphors.

Beckett was a generous correspondent; writing letters seems to have come more easily than writing fiction. Even when he was flooded with fan mail after winning the Nobel Prize for Literature in 1969, he dutifully answered each congratulatory letter himself. *The Letters of Samuel Beckett*, published in four volumes by Cambridge University Press, select only a small fraction of the more than 15,000 that have survived, under Beckett's restriction that only passages bearing on his work should be made public. The editors interpreted the rule widely, and the volumes are rich with Beckett's sensibility and his connection with a wide array of friends. Some crucial relationships are altogether missing. Beckett must have destroyed the letters he wrote before the age of 23, including those to his parents May and Bill Beckett, as well as the entire correspondence between himself and his life partner, Suzanne Deschevaux-Dumesnil. Very few letters, none in print, are available between 1941 and 1944, when he and Suzanne fled from the

Gestapo after the betrayal of Beckett's underground resistance cell, and hid in the southern mountain village of Roussillon until the end of the war.

When I juxtapose letters with published works, I am not primarily using them as sources of biographical information that might identify this or that character or situation in Beckett's work. Rather, I am calling attention to two kinds of writing that resonate with one another. Both are self-presentations to an audience, whether adapted for a single known correspondent or for an unknown public, and both have fictional aspects. Beckett's letters are full of sentences and observations that capture characteristic gestures of thought and feeling, and set up dialogues with his published work.

The original versions of Beckett's work were often written in French, raising questions of translation. The fictions before and during World War II were composed in English, and include *Dream of Fair to Middling Women* (long unpublished), *More Pricks Than Kicks*, *Murphy*, and *Watt*. After the war, in an effort to declutter his style and distance himself from his Irish roots, he began to write in French. His great postwar flowering in French produced the novels *Molloy*, *Malone Dies*, and *The Unnamable*, as well as the play *Waiting for Godot*. By the later 1950s, prompted by invitations to write radio plays for the BBC, he began composing again in English. From then on, he moved between languages, depending on the work he had in mind.

Because Beckett translated his own works in both directions, or revised translations begun by others, reading for small shifts of style in a translated work is less problematic than it would otherwise be. Like any translator, he had to make accommodations that might recapture the spirit and idiom in which the original was written. Although I will not pursue questions of translation in this book, readers should be aware that a prior text in French lies behind certain of the works I will discuss. The same goes for the letters, some of which were written in French or German. The Cambridge edition has helpfully reproduced those letters in both the original and in English.

My chapters concentrate on prose works and a few prose-like performance pieces. They are not intended to give a full account of Beckett's career, and may be read as individual pieces, each spotlighting a certain phase of his productive life. My own reading and writing path helped to determine the chapter order, as I found myself halted by certain works, compelled to sink in and figure out a way to explain them to myself. The book begins at the end, so to speak, because I was first moved to write about Beckett when I encountered two works composed in his seventies. The play *That Time* and the prose work *Company* spoke to my longstanding interest in memory and the pitfalls of autobiography, but they also charmed and impressed me with their poetic force and their intriguing narrative forms. The middle chapters are roughly chronological, moving along the path that Beckett cleared as he made his way forward in fiction. He always demanded the most difficult literary tasks from himself: each new work had to find a newly adequate form, and burrow further into the internal landscape of the creative mind. The fifth and final chapter draws together Beckett's rhythms of attachment and loss, as he writes about the deaths of others and human relationships with cherished objects.

Like other brilliant innovators, Beckett has been interpreted and reinterpreted by literary critics ever since he came to prominence in the 1950s. Each new generation creates a different Beckett to meet the concerns and fashions of its era. If some twentieth-century critics saw in his work a search for an authentic self, more recent ones might depict him through postmodernist lenses as a writer who undermines the possibility that we inhabit anything that could be called a self. My own reading finds Beckett more interested in the interplay among different voices in a single mind than he is in any philosophy of subjectivity. With an ear exquisitely tuned to the history of literary styles and genres, he had little truck with attempts to theorize or explain his positions. The much quoted final line of *Watt*, "no symbols where none intended," mocks those who want to impose layers of meaning on his fictions. The phrase also turns its irony on the notion that any-one, including the author himself, can ascertain for sure what a literary passage "intended."

Honoring Beckett's fierce insistence on the integrity of his writing as it stood on the page, I will not engage at all thoroughly with the mass of critical opinion and analysis that surrounds his art. The chapters to follow are attempts to fashion a Samuel Beckett of my own.

WRITING MEMORY

My life, my life, now I speak of it as something over, now as of a
joke which still goes on, and it is neither, for at the same time it is
over and it goes on, and is there any tense for that?

—Samuel Beckett, *Molloy*

When Beckett began composing *Molloy* in 1947, he abandoned
the third-person narrators of his previous novels *Murphy*,
Watt, and *Mercier and Camier*. Molloy's story is told mostly in the
first-person past-tense mode common to autobiography and
autobiographical fiction. Beckett was already conscious that the
form could not convey what it is like to pass through experience
that continues to be remembered and replayed in the present. As
Molloy queries, "is there any tense for that?"[1] Thirty years later,
nearing the end of his writing life, Beckett experimented with
forms of narrative that could get at the workings of memory as he
understood them. Especially in the performance piece *That Time*
(1976) and the prose work *Company* (1980), Beckett found ways to
convey the strangeness of memory as it repeats and revises itself
in a human head.

Memories of the past can arrive with a sense of incredulity in
later life. As time goes on, my own past becomes more and more
mysterious to me. A scene pops up in my head as I'm going to
sleep, or making use of some household object I've had for a long

time. I have to wonder: was that clueless young person really the same as the one I now inhabit? Why does this tiny but embarrassing childhood episode keep coming back? Did something like that really happen, or is it an image my memory mind has somehow revised and recycled? These are puzzles that Beckett explores with tenderness, sadness, and skepticism. I first found myself captivated by *That Time* and *Company* because they speak of the pleasure and discomfort in fragmentary images of the past that appear without warning, laden with vivid mixtures of emotion.

Brief scenes that seem to be memories of Beckett's youth in and around Dublin show up here and there throughout his postwar work. *That Time* and *Company* evoke the process of memory itself. They are especially tantalizing because they refuse the pronoun "I" while offering relatively prolonged scenes set in the past. Readers who focus just on the lyrical memory scenes are apt to consider them nostalgic, and to accept them as late-life representations of Beckett's youth in Ireland. But the framework in which they appear is just as important, and just as moving. In both works, a silent listener is subjected to a series of supposedly external voices that seem to be telling him about previous incarnations of himself. The voices, each differently inflected, distribute the actions of the memory mind into separate characters.

Questioning the false promises of the pronoun "I" was always an important element in Beckett's writing. In English, the stroke and sound of the pronoun has a special singularity, as if it initiates the line of the self through time. When I taught courses in autobiography and autobiographical fiction, I wanted to engage my students with the non-identity within the I-word, which deceptively blurs past selves with present narrators. It's never simple to disentangle the story line from the conscious or unconscious motives or designs of the teller who looks back and shapes the story for present purposes. Beckett's self-conscious art spoke happily to my previous fascination with such elusive matters of narrative.

The word "identity," in all its shifting psychological and cultural meanings, has always bothered me. The gaps between my social self, my writing voice, and my internal mono/dialogue often feel wide. "I" covers over the multiplicities of being that human beings experience every day, as we play different roles in different places; move between silence and speech, solitude and sociability; observe ourselves in action or in thought; recall and distort past moments. What we call identity rests on an alleged continuity of memory, yet the actual activity of memory in daily life is anything but continuous.

Chronologically organized autobiographical and biographical narratives sew the subject together in ways that are necessarily half-invented. As early as 1871, 16-year-old Arthur Rimbaud remarked in a letter, "Je est un autre" (I is another). Beckett took up that idea and elaborated it endlessly. He can belabor the unstable relationship between "he" and "I" in ways that can strike some readers as arcane game-playing. To my mind, such passages adorn the surfaces of something real about writing: the inevitable gap between narrative and the person from whom it issues. Sometimes I reread some of my previous writing and think, "Who wrote that?" The notion of a discontinuous and multiple set of tendencies within each human being comes more naturally to me than any simple claim of identity. I'm also intrigued by Beckett's mind-twisting pronoun play because I have always veiled my own auto-biographical impulses in narratives about historical figures. Just as Beckett's narrators and characters serve as surrogates for different aspects of himself, his writing, for the purposes of this book, serves as a self-exploration for me. The "I" who appears in this book is, in the end, a created character that expresses some aspects of myself and silences others.

A charming episode from *Watt* (composed 1941–45) makes a telling prelude to the memory works of Beckett's seventies. The Galls, father and son, turn up at Mr. Knott's house to tune the piano, leaving the servant Watt in considerable doubt and speculation. Should he let them in? Which one of them is the actual tuner? Or is the father training the son to take over for him? Is the father deaf as well as blind? Once the tuners are finished, Watt overhears a perfectly Beckettian dialogue between son and father:

> The mice have returned, he said.
> The elder said nothing. Watt wondered if he had heard.
> Nine dampers remain, said the younger, and an equal
>   number of hammers.
> Not corresponding, I hope, said the elder.
> In one case, said the younger.
> The elder had nothing to say to this.
> The strings are in flitters, said the younger.
> The elder had nothing to say to this either.
> The piano is doomed, in my opinion, said the younger.
> The piano-tuner also, said the elder.
> The pianist also, said the younger.   (*Watt*, 72)

That piano could not possibly have been tuned at all. Watt is puzzled. The external narrator takes over, asserting that this incident resembles all of Watt's experiences during his mysterious servitude in Mr. Knott's house.

> It resembled them in the sense that it was not ended, when it was past, but continued to unfold, in Watt's head, from beginning to

end, over and over again, the complex connexions of its lights and shadows, the passing from silence to sound and from sound to silence, the stillness before the movement and the stillness after, the quickenings and retardings, the approaches and the separations, all the shifting detail of its march and ordinance, according to the irrecoverable caprice of its taking place.[2]

These lyrical abstractions turn the incident from deadpan comedy into a dazzling sequence of light, sound, and motion, as if to evoke the sensory brain processes that transform an observed event into a memory sequence. The original, randomly encountered episode is "irrecoverable." For Watt, the replayed memory sequences remain uncomfortable because they are full of doubt. He cannot know whether the event actually happened, or how to place it in time.

> So Watt did not know what had happened. He did not care, to do him justice, what had happened. But he felt the need to think that such and such a thing had happened then, the need to be able to say, when the scene began to unroll its sequences, Yes, I remember, that is what happened then.   (Watt, 74)

The memory has its own dynamic, separate from Watt's will: it unrolls in his head like a film, without his participation. "He did not care, to do him justice, what had happened," brings the twist and the smile. This is the joy of Beckett, I think, the joke that splits Watt's anxious need to master his past from his actual willingness to live with doubt.

The play Not I (1972) was Beckett's first experiment with a dramatic form that separates memory from the I-word. Its jerkily hysterical monologue of past pain is spoken by an onstage female Mouth—an eerily embodied voice—who represents a "vehement refusal to relinquish third person."[3] Interrupted five times by an apparently internal questioner, she denies each time that her subject is anyone other than a third-person "she." Her denial emphasizes the strength of her need to distance herself from early pain, while she is forcibly compelled to express it. Her past intrudes without her invitation or consent, taking over her being as a symptom of trauma.

For *That Time* Beckett invented a form that captures the way more ordinary memories recur and expand as they gather further associations. The play divides its memory paragraphs among three alternating voices, A, C, and B (usually in that order), who address a silent and minimally responsive listener as "you." The voices come from offstage, while the listener's face hovers above stage level, displaying life only through the sound of his breath and the opening and shutting of his eyes. The emotions expressed on the actor's face were essential to Beckett, who worried that the face had a disproportionally small role. He told his American producer Alan Schneider that he had "now come to accept its remoteness and stillness—apart from certain precise eye movements, breath just audible in silences and final smile—as essential to the piece & dramatically of value."[4] He refused to allow a radio performance in German: "In my opinion *Damals* as a radio play is out of the question because of the loss of the picture, i.e. half of the whole thing! The listening face is an inextricable part. Otherwise it would no longer be a play, but only an aimless voice without any suspense" (*Letters*, 4:443). After going to such trouble to separate the memory scenes from the listener, Beckett was anxious to show that the relationship between a person and his memories is, above all, an emotional dialogue between different parts of the self.

Each of the three voices is assigned a different memory scene, which shifts, develops, and gradually overlaps with the others.

Paragraphs appear in run-on style without punctuation, evading the rational ordering implied by grammatical sentences. The play depends on the performer to voice the phrases in a lyrical and intelligible way. Reading it on the page, you have to slow down to hear the voicing of each sentence or fragment as it emerges from the unstopped flow of language.

In his stage note Beckett writes, "Moments of one and the same voice A B C relay one another without solution of continuity—apart from the two 10-second breaks. Yet the switch from one to another must be clearly faintly perceptible."[5] The arrangement implies that individual memory scenes live on separate tracks in one mind, replaying themselves with additions, subtractions, or emendations. Though they all address themselves to a single "you," Beckett will not put them into a single chronological sequence that might constitute an "I." Nonetheless, as the play moves along, the voices begin to intertwine, creating a recognizable being.

Beckett's stage note quotes the phrase "without solution of continuity" from his own early work, the essay on Proust he had composed in 1930. There, he had ventured a theory of memory that transcends chronology. It's not based on deliberate recall, such as when we look through a photo album, but on what he calls involuntary memory. This happens when a subject is suddenly overtaken by a moment from the past that is vividly present, as Proust is precipitated into his childhood by the smell and taste of the madeleine. "As though the figure of Time could be represented by an endless series of parallels, his life is switched over to another line and proceeds, without any solution of continuity, from that remote moment of his past when his grandmother stooped over his distress."[6] I try to grasp this image of the past as a train switching tracks to run alongside the train of the present.

There are no cars connecting one train with the other, but present and past run in intimate parallel for the duration of the memory. "Without solution of continuity" seems to mean that one could not hitch all the memory tracks together to construct a single life-train running on a single track.

The play's title words, *That Time*, beautifully evoke the difficulty of getting straight what actually happened in the past, and when. "Remember that time we climbed Mt. Tallac?" I might say to my brother. "When was that? Would that have been before our father died?" *That Time* concerns a memory of memory-chasing, when the listener has returned to Ireland on a last journey to see whether his old childhood haunts are still there. It begins like this:

> A: that time you went back that last time to look was the ruin still there where you hid as a child when was that [Eyes close.] grey day took the eleven to the end of the line and on from there no no trams all gone long ago that time you went back to look was the ruin still there where you hid as a child that last time not a tram left in the place only the old rails when was that. (*That Time*, 388)

The subject's eyes close as if to remember, but he remembers "that time" wrong, conflating the times he took the tram home with that last time, when the trams were "all gone long ago." Did Beckett's trams recall those Proustian tracks of time, now revised in his three-track system of voices? The writing in the passage brings to mind a different metaphor of memories as palimpsests, with each mental reoccurrence of a scene from the past layered upon the previous one. As the recalled scene is altered or distorted over time, each occurrence is really a memory of previous memories, though some trace of the original event remains. According to recent memory theory, persistent repetitions of particular memory images probably depend on the intensity of emotion attached to them.[7]

In Beckett's play the subject never succeeds in returning to the ruin itself, because the origins of a memory are inaccessible. Revisiting a known place at a later time, even if familiar objects have not disappeared or crumbled, is entirely different from being there as a child for whom the place is an unquestioned part of ordinary life. It cannot be the same place. But the voice of A continues on its mission to paint the place anew, by building up his imaginative associations with the old ruin.

The discontinuities of memory come up against a countervailing pull of narrative, as the outlines of a single being start to emerge in A's voice. The tendencies of the remembered child begin to merge with the traits of the visiting adult. The child who hides in the old ruin is already attracted to isolation and things "all gone long ago." In his hideout he entertains himself by "talking to yourself who else out loud imaginary conversations there was childhood for you ten or eleven on a stone among the giant nettles making it up now one voice now another till you were hoarse and they all sounded the same" (That Time, 390). "Making it up now one voice then another" links the child with the author of the play, and with his older revisiting self. As A's sections end, the speaker is wrapped in a tangible mantle of memory, his father's old green greatcoat. He shares his mental life with the child who tells his stories aloud to himself in the old ruin. Waiting for the night ferry that will take him out of Ireland, he talks out loud despite the stares of passers-by, "making yourself all up again for the millionth time forgetting it all" (That Time, 394). The quest for a physical reconnection with the past is quickly abandoned in disgust: "not a curse for the old scenes the old names" (That Time, 389).

What matters is making up every memory anew, as if for the first time.

The scenes assigned to voices B and C are diffused with similar blends of isolation and connection through memory. B's story concerns two lovers sitting wide apart on a stone bench, never touching or moving closer but murmuring vows of love as they gaze separately out on a continually shifting natural landscape. Eventually the scene is dismissed as an erotic fantasy, "just one of those things you kept making up to keep the void out" (*That Time*, 390). Lingering on a memory and playing out its changes helps fend off a confrontation with meaninglessness. It's a bare statement of what had always been a central motif in Beckett's writing.

C's part is set in an urban world where a lonely adolescent tries to hide in public places. When it rains, he enters public buildings—museum, post office, library—when he thinks no one is looking. Once inside, he suffers the self-conscious shame of being seen to be alone and in need of shelter. This voice includes a riff on the well-worn notion of "never being the same" after some experience. It adamantly rejects the notion of turning points that change the direction of a life, as they often do in conventional autobiography. Life is a mess in which past, present, and future can't be distinguished. No linear progression can be discerned: how can you say you were never the same if you can't say how you were before? The never-the-same fantasy gets a sarcastic put-down: "never the same but the same as what for God's sake did you ever say I to yourself in your life come on now" (*That Time*, 390). No solution of continuity there; no one is saying I to himself. And don't we often address ourselves as "you" in our minds?

Without ever saying so, the three interwoven voices create a portrait of a recognizable being through time, whose prides, fears, talents, and humiliations are alluring and discomforting in the act of looking back. Then it is over: the play ends in dust and silence, as if its spoken words have decayed like the ruins of old Irish haunts. Nothing remains except a final line stating the essential life rhythm that links the three voices and their tales: "come and gone." Memories, like most other things in Beckett's world, light up and then disappear. Not without a trace: the half-nostalgic, half-defiant being who tells stories to himself in creative isolation lingers as a multiplex portrait of a single and singular person.

Perhaps because *That Time* rings so deeply with Irish intonations, Beckett had a lot of trouble making a French translation. In a 1977 letter to Ruby Cohn, he merged his difficulty with the hint of a new work in English. "Have a rough draft of *That Time* in French, but loss so great not the heart so far to finalize... Tried to get going again in English to see me through, say for company, but broke down. But must somehow" (*Letters*, 4:457). In the last months of 1977, he was drafting a preliminary version of the English prose work *Company*. "I try to write only to keep me company but am finding it even worse than my own and hope soon to desist," Beckett declared to the Irish poet Brian Coffey from his solitary writing cottage in Ussy-sur-Marne. He liked the witticism, and repeated it some days later to Ruby Cohn: "*Company* proving the worst possible. Shall end up by preferring my own" (*Letters*, 4:476).

A prose work of about forty pages, *Company* is far trickier than *That Time*. Like the play, it involves a silent, inert subject who hears a voice that talks or murmurs to him, addressing him as "you" as he lies on his back in the dark. The voice presents scenes that feel directly autobiographical, this time involving specific memories of mother, father, lover, and child. These sections, which occupy the smaller portion of the narrative, are sometimes extracted and discussed as if they were accounts of Beckett's early life. There is no way to tell whether they are recalled, invented, or both. Beckett often plants guidelines for the reader on the first pages of his prose works; in this case we are warned, "But by far the greater part of what is said cannot be verified."[8]

Taken in concert, the scenes from the past create a portrait of a sensitive, self-conscious boy whose yearning for close connection is repeatedly baffled, through the mother's failure to accept his sensibility, through the death of his beloved father, or through his own childish failures. Nothing like this is ever said, of course. The emotional power of the scenes lies in the evocative details that enclose feelings in images. At most, they convey ongoing pain in the declaration, "you have never forgotten." Yet in this late work Beckett loosens the reins on emotion that had confined earlier outbreaks of similar scenes.

One memory paragraph describes a young child walking hand in hand with his mother. In *Company*, the course of the walk is described in loving detail, until the child attempts to charm and impress his mother by breaking their silence to ask if the sky is more distant, or closer, than it appears. "For some reason you could never fathom this question must have angered her exceedingly. For she shook off your little hand and made you a cutting retort you have never forgotten" (*Company*, 6). Clearly, it's the mother who is more distant than she appears. Her unfathomable negation of her child's creative curiosity is the confusing blow that continues to replay itself in his mind. The scene itself is a replay of two more defensive passages from Beckett's earlier work. In his story "The End" a romantic mood of wonder in a "small boy" is abruptly punctured by his mother's shocking response: "The earth makes a sound as of sighs and the last drops fall from the empty, cloudless sky. A small boy, stretching out his hands and looking up at the blue sky, asked his mother how such a thing was possible. Fuck off, she said."[9] And later, from *Malone Dies*:

> I said, The sky is further away than you think, is it not, mama? It was without malice. I was simply thinking of all the leagues that separated me from it. She replied, to me her son, It is precisely as far away as it seems to be. She was right. But at the time I was aghast.

This narrator protects himself by asserting the purity of his motives, as if he were still under his mother's disapproving sway. Feeling "aghast" is limited to the past, and Malone quickly veers away into landscape images, only to return with second thoughts: "My mother? Perhaps it is just another story, told to me by some one who found it funny. The stories I was told, at one time! And all funny, not one not funny."[10] The moment turns into one of those family stories that deflect intense feeling in humorous recollection, becoming bits of family lore removed from the child's experience. The double negatives of "not one not funny," pretend to declare it funny when it felt anything but funny. Whether a scene just like this occurred remains in doubt. It's only in *Company*—written after the death of his actual mother—that Beckett creates a richer context and asserts its lasting power. For me, the repeated scenes speak of a sensitive child whose pride is readily hurt, and whose adult memory can't help but worry over moments of humiliation or unsympathetic misunderstanding.

Company's pictures of the father are ample and loving, but they also include private discomforts that leave a residue of mixed feeling. A long description of the father's daylong flight into the hills to avoid his wife's prolonged labor in childbirth could only be a revised version of some much-repeated family story, if it's not an outright fiction. When a maid finds the father hiding in his car and tells him "it was over at last," the narrator repeats "Over!" in mock horror or dismay (*Company*, 8). Someone's life is just beginning; a new childhood and motherhood and fatherhood have come into being, and nothing about all this will ever be over, Beckett knows, until long after their deaths. He sometimes imagined birth as the kiss of death, as in Pozzo's line from *Waiting for Godot*: "They give birth astride of a grave, the light gleams an instant, then it's night once more."[11] But that tiny exclamation, "Over!" carries the weight of all the living that must be done before the night falls.

In a different memory frozen with tension, the father waits for the boy to jump from a high diving board into the rockbound sea. The child's fearful hesitation is amplified by his self-conscious awareness of nearby strangers' eyes trained on him. As the scene goes on, the distance between the memory voice and the listening subject narrows, until the listener is participating so fully in past sensations that time is momentarily erased. "You look down to the loved trusted face. He calls to you to jump. He calls, Be a brave boy. The round red face. The thick moustache. The greying hair. The swell sways it under and sways it up again. The far call again, Be a brave boy" (*Company*, 11). The wave washing over the father's face is like a memory blotted out and then recovered. The listener hears the far call in the present, as he lies on his back in the dark.

The present-day merge with memory continues when he recollects his vision of a very distant mountain from his solitary boyhood hiding place. "The first time you told them you were derided. All you had seen was a cloud. So now you hoard it in your heart with the rest" (*Company*, 15). The child's belief in his own vision is cherished in private against the common-sense judgments of his family, connecting him with the child in *That Time*. The present-day listener strains his own closed eyes again and again, until he sees the mountain emerge again out of the distance of time. The final lyrical memory in *Company* also links the listener lying on his back with a youth lying on his back under a tree, gazing into the eyes of a girl who lies at a right angle to him. In the present, he can feel the fringe of her hair on his face. While the beauty and flexibility of Beckett's descriptive prose can feel like nostalgia, the moments themselves are so laced with tension and unresolved conflict that they can't be called yearnings for a lost time.

One moment stands out among the series depicting oblique human relationships: a little drama with a hedgehog that happens to cross the child's path one day. He glows with self-congratulation for the kind effort he's made on its behalf when he secures the creature in an unused shed with the door wedged open, and some worms "to tide it over." The more he thinks it over, the more he worries that he may have interfered with a perfectly good life. "Days if not weeks passed before you could bring yourself to return to the hutch. You have never forgotten what you found then. The mush. The stench" (*Company*, 19). In these terse words I feel the horror and revulsion that lingers after an act that feels like generosity, but causes pain or even death. Beckett's lifelong fear of hurting other living creatures haunts the brief paragraph.

"A voice comes to one in the dark. Imagine." These sentences stand alone as the first paragraph of *Company*, linking the one lying on his back in the dark with the author's imperative to himself, as if he were saying, "You've heard a voice in your head. Start imagining the story." If the recalled child of memory is marked by self-consciousness, the story surrounding those past scenes is even more fully committed to teasing out self-conscious acts of narration. "The dark" that encloses both the silent listener and the narrator links the inner space of imagination and memory in both. Reading this part of the novella, I found myself delighting in the way Beckett undoes the assumptions that so many of us have dutifully conveyed to students: that the telling voice on the page is the narrator, who must be kept separate from the author, about whom we must not speak. The narrator's voice must also be kept separate from the quoted voices of characters, which inhabit yet another narrative dimension. Yet when we talk informally, we call the book's voices by the author's name, as I am doing here.

The voice that tells memories to the "you" lying in the dark is not alone. Someone else is on the scene: "And in another dark or in the same another, devising it all for company. Quick leave him" (*Company*, 3). *The same another*: like the "one and the same voice," divided into three, that tells *That Time*, the split imagination is a single entity proliferating in different voices that react to one another. This deviser brings a series of new perspectives. He refers to the supine listener as "he," and comments on the activities of the memory voice. He throws out many possible ways to describe aspects of the listener's being, and the configuration of his body in space. He often wonders out loud whether a different way of imagining that body would make the narrative more interesting or keep it going. These suggestions, ventured in the hope of making additions to company, are often rejected as quickly as they appear.

Who or what is this deviser? He is mentioned only to be instantly disavowed: "Quick leave him." But who says that? Is it the one who organizes the writing behind the scenes—that is, the author? Or is the devisor the narrator, who directs the flow of the telling, while another voice, perhaps the author's, interjects his own ideas? Finally, if one or both of these sources is devising for company, does that mean for a reading audience or to give himself company—or both?

As I puzzled over these questions, I concluded that Beckett was calling attention to the various parts of a writer that are activated by the process of writing. What are the differences, if any, between a character, a narrator, and a living author who hides behind the scenes? I was reminded of a short story by Jorge Luis Borges called "Borges and I" (1960), which Beckett could have known. The "Borges" of the title is the public author, while the "I" is the living man whose interests and experiences are transformed into literature signed by "Borges." "I" feels that he has given over his life to "Borges," yet the distinctions between them keep slipping and sliding. The final sentence, "I am not sure which of us it is that's writing this page," could serve as an epigraph for *Company*.[12] Beckett, however, makes a more complex drama in which the elements of writing—imagination, invention, memory, author, narrator, reader—are braided together in a way that keeps the reader switching gears from paragraph to paragraph. This can be dizzying and frustrating, but I found that it gradually evolved into a moving portrait of authorship.

Beckett's tricky narrative led me to consider my own experience of writing. I can't put my finger on just who arranges that one sentence will follow another, or what parts of my brain and heart keep revising what's just appeared on the page. My sentences look back at me from the page, offering company, and asking for response. My critical ear hears the sentences, prompting deletions, questions about what I meant, frustration, or pleasure in something that finally came out right. My reading takes hold of literary passages I like, and wants to meet them with understanding words of my own. Beckett's remarkable technique both conjures up formal distinctions among living writer, contriving author, and narrative voice, and makes it difficult to maintain them.

Early on the tricky voice assumes that the memory voice keeps harping on the same old scenes because it wants to make the silent listener own up to them. Is Beckett teasing biographers and journalists who want him to confess that his memory scenes are accurate accounts of his own youth? As in *Watt*, there's a floating desire to attach a memory securely to an "I" with an acknowledged past. "To confess, Yes I remember. Perhaps even to have a voice. To murmur, Yes I remember. What an addition to company that would be! A voice in the first person singular. Murmuring now and then, Yes I remember" (*Company*, 9). While Watt thinks he wants only the reassurance of knowing something definite, the later voice is tempted by something different: it's writing to give itself company. If the listening subject were to enter the scene as a speaking "I," it jokes, there would be another person for its own entertainment. As usual, the joke has its serious side. For the solitary writer, creating a new character is a way to provide himself with another being, who can offer expansions of company.

The I-word pops up again in a paragraph that just increases my bafflement about how many presences we are dealing with:

> And whose voice asking this? Who asks, Whose voice asking this? And answers His soever who devises it all. In the same dark as his creature or in another. For company. Who asks in the end, Who asks? And in the end answers as above? And adds long after to himself, Unless another still. Nowhere to be found. Nowhere to be sought. The unthinkable last of all. Unnamable. Last person. I. Quick leave him. (*Company*, 15)

Although he is nowhere to be found, this unnamable mystery person has to be the writer/author who hides inside the deviser/ narrator's questions and answers. The authorial first-person pronoun acquires a new label, "last person." He appears only to disappear, but he is there. While the deviser is given a mock god-like power of creation, "His soever who devises it all," the "yet another" behind the scenes is, grammatically and otherwise, a person. "Devising figments to temper his nothingness. Quick leave him. Pause and again in panic to himself, Quick leave him" (*Company*, 30).

Beckett's wonderful comedy, this panicked shying away from evidence of a human being who writes to allay his nothingness, feels to me like one of the most genuinely autobiographical flashes in *Company*. The moment quickly brings more admissions, as the deviser is named as one of the writer's figments. And it isn't long before the blended creator is further merged with the physical being of the one lying on his back. The author/deviser has been wondering whether to vary the story by setting him to crawl in some obsessional pattern—would that add to company? And "Can the crawling creator crawling in the same create dark as his creature create while crawling?" (*Company*, 34). Beckett must have enjoyed that tongue-twister, as he merges all three characters into one. At a moment when creator/crawler/listener loses faith in his project, his desire for company revives his need to keep inventing.

The gradual blending of listener, writer, and narrator also shows up in sequence featuring a familiar Beckett protagonist, an old man walking, clad in the father's long greatcoat. He is introduced to the one lying on his back as one of his memories: a writer's earlier creations are just as much part of his personal past as anything else. Unlike the other memories, this one is accorded a history threading through a number of different paragraphs, forging links between the memory and the writing tracks of *Company*.

This walker is openly a figure for the writer. He is getting old; his words have covered many pages and territories, but he cannot add them all up into a sequential life. His steps get shorter and slower, like Beckett's late work. He passes the time by making up compulsive games: counting footsteps or calculating the passage of shadows on the face of a watch. As his story opens, the walking figure listens to his footfalls in the silence, counting his steps to ascertain the precise distance covered. Yet after he stops to make the calculation, he resumes his walk, side by side with the father's shade, "from nought anew" (*Company*, 8). His urge to measure the path of his life through time gives way to the recognition that each moment has to be reckoned as a new beginning. Nonetheless, the figure goes through the familiar Beckett stages of deterioration and loss. He endures the seasons and covers a lot of territory; the companionship of his father's shade disappears, along with his physical mobility. At the last he is supine, identical with the "you" on his back, and merged with all the other voices and characters of *Company*.

The endings of Beckett's later works tend to be farewells to the act of writing that has brought them into being. The writing is ending, but the life in question, however attenuated, has not yet ended. Molloy's question about the right tense for memory now lights up in a different way, suggesting the distinction between the life force that carries a piece of writing and the human existence it leaves behind: "My life, my life, now I speak of it as something over, now as of a joke which still goes on, and it is neither, for at the same time it is over and it goes on, and is there any tense for that?" (*Three Novels*, 31). As the narrative of *Company* winds down, we get a brief glimpse of the composite writer awakening from the dark dream of creation. "Numb with the woes of your kind you raise none the less your head from off your hands and open your eyes" (*Company*, 38). His emotional weariness and his physical presence in space are palpable.

At the end the subject is no longer creator or deviser or listener but a teller with more ancient roots, a "fabler," a single being that encompasses the writer and all his voices, including the memories. As he bids a final goodbye to *Company*, the fabler begins to dissolve. The speaking voice now addresses him as one who labors "in vain," whose "every inane word a little nearer to the last." The final lines attempt to reconcile the fabler to the loss of company: "And how better in the end labour lost and silence. And you as you always were. Alone." The fabler, like the walker, will have to begin all over if he is to regain the companionship of writing. What has come to an end in this piece is now "labour lost," work separated from him and lost to him. It's a familiar feeling, shared by many who come to the end of a writing project and prepare to send it away. Sequestered in its own line and space, Beckett's "Alone" captures the sense of abandonment I feel during such moments, when everything that has filled my imagination for months and years begins to drain away.

The need to begin anew led Beckett directly to the short play called *Rockaby*. Written just after *Company* in 1980, it performs a lovely coda to the "not-I" sequence. Again, a speaker acts as an off-stage memory voice for a dying woman who rocks onstage in her rocking chair. The voice murmurs the same phrases, with additions and variations, over and over, creating a kind of incantatory poem. It begins

> till in the end
> the day came

in the end came
close of a long day
when she said
to herself
whom else
time she stopped
time she stopped.[13]

Repeated in italics, that last phrase deepens the impossible desire to take charge of one's own ending, and gives voice to a more urgent tone that may reside within the silent woman herself. While she waits for her death to arrive, the speaking voice recalls her previous phase, when she still wanted to see and be seen by some creature like herself. She had been upstairs looking out her window, hoping to see another being in a window across the way. All the blinds there are pulled down, signifying death. Finally, one blind opens. She closes her own, goes downstairs, and sits in the rocking chair her mother had rocked and died in. She is now resigned, the voice tells her, to being entirely isolated, "her own other/own other living soul" (*Rockaby*, 441). The repetition of "own other" is breathtaking, reminding me that she is, after all, still there for herself. Then her eyes shut down and she rocks off. To death? To sleep? It's difficult to read *Rockaby* without feeling it as a gently forgiving eulogy for May Beckett.

In closing this chapter, I ask myself why I am so drawn to Beckett's decision to write his most personal memory work without using the first-person pronoun. He had certainly done wonders with first-person fiction in the great novel trilogy he began with *Molloy*. The most direct answer may lie in what happened recently when, with Beckett in mind, I tried to describe a few persistent memories of my own. I found myself writing in the third person, because my young self *was*, by now, a third person, imagined from a distance as if she were a visible character in a film. She could not have put herself into the temporal or visual contexts that came naturally to me, so many decades later. I also felt instinctively that I wanted the distance so that emotion could rise from the spaces between the words. That child could not articulate the names of the feelings attached to the scenes, and I had no desire to put words into her mouth.

Beckett's reluctance to write directly about his past, and his care to avoid the display of confession or nostalgia, led him to enclose memory feelings in formal arrangements that place them at a certain remove. When he separates memories from the subjects they belong to, and divides the components of the writing process into separate characters, he is also exercising the poetic gifts that weave together all the various parts of that discontinuous self. His ingenious portrait of writing as an internal drama that creates company for the writer has become a cherished part of my consciousness as I make sentences and paragraphs of my own.

BELACQUA AND MR. BECKETT

He has turned out to be simply not that kind of person.

—Samuel Beckett, *Dream of Fair to Middling Women*

Had Beckett not become famous for his postwar novels and plays, I would probably not be writing this chapter about his earliest efforts at fiction. The unpublished *Dream of Fair to Middling Women*, the stories in *More Pricks Than Kicks*, and the largely ignored *Murphy* were written during Beckett's troubled twenties, when he was struggling painfully to extricate himself from his family's expectations and from the academic career he'd prepared for at Trinity College Dublin. After he had found his distinctive voice, he preferred to leave the early work behind. It was only late in life that he gave reluctant permission for *Dream of Fair to Middling Women* to be published after his death.

As I read these fictions along with the rather anguished letters from this period, I grew interested in the links between Beckett's attempts to pull away from the provincial Irish society he deplored and his tussle with the traditional novel form. As a literary scholar, Beckett was well aware of the resources he inherited from both English and French novel traditions, and he was determined to shake them off, to attempt something entirely new. But he could not do that without first staging a battle in prose, in which he relied on, mocked, parodied, and argued with the very conventions he wanted to leave behind.

I have spent a large part of my life watching those conventions at work in nineteenth- and twentieth-century British fiction, so I may find more personal entertainment in Beckett's adolescent literary antics than others would. In truth, I find them moving, because they attest to a genuine and lifelong—and of course impossible—struggle for freedom from the rules and assumptions that young Beckett scorned as practices that kept him hemmed in by others' expectations. His deep resistance to being defined by other people, or by ordinary social rituals and professional roles, extended to the creation of his invented characters and narrators. His particular anguish lay in his knotty relationship with his mother, who expressed her intense love by trying to make her son over into her image of bourgeois Irish Protestant success.

Skepticism about literary character was on Beckett's mind from the start. His early novels feature protagonists whose most fervent desire is to fly away from worldly commitments and diffuse themselves in some inaccessible realm elsewhere. They refuse to see themselves as characters who have been formed by the social circumstances they were dealt at birth. Both the narrators who tell the tales and the actors they describe are creatures with blurred boundaries, who—if they are worthy—refuse to stay consistently "in character."

Belacqua, borrowed from Dante's *Divine Comedy*, is the name Beckett gave to his first protagonists. The original Belacqua appears in Canto IV of the *Purgatorio*, where Dante encounters him on the steep climb through Purgatory and recognizes him as an old acquaintance, a sardonic Florentine lute-maker known for his laziness. Belacqua, as indolent as ever, is now lingering under a pre-purgatorial rock that is neither on earth nor properly in purgatory. When Dante asks him why he does not hike up to the gates to begin the process of repentance and redemption, he answers "O frate, l'andar su che porta?" ("Brother, what is the use of going up?"). He does not think the angel at the gate will let him pass. "The heavens must first wheel about me, waiting outside, as long as in my lifetime, because I put off good sighs to the last."[1]

The appeal of Belacqua in limbo struck me forcefully when I read the passage in Dante. It gave Beckett a name for the indolent, directionless, antisocial character who thrashes around in social settings and relationships. But it's more than just a clever allusion or a tribute to Beckett's love for Dante. Belacqua's afterlife is a mental reliving of his entire life course, from the safe distance of pre-purgatory. I often think that Beckett himself could hardly experience his own acts, words, and feelings without immediately stepping away to re-see them from a different perspective. He was well aware that he was always observing himself from an imaginary afar. In May 1934, Beckett wrote a long letter in German to his cousin Morris Sinclair, including an excuse for his failure to answer a letter from Morris's father. "It is a strange feeling to step back instinctively well away from oneself, and observe oneself as through a keyhole. Strange, yes, and utterly unsuitable for letter writing."[2] Beckett's image of a suspicious detective who spies on himself from behind closed doors may glance at the analytic treatment he was undergoing at that time, but it was, as he wrote, instinctive, and would become the basis for his art. That acute self-consciousness nurtured both his self-torment and his genius. During the years before he managed to establish permanent residence in his preferred elsewhere, Paris, watching himself was also freighted with an uncomfortable blend of intellectual arrogance and self-disgust.

Dream of Fair to Middling Women is full of its author's troubles. He and his parents were enduring a prolonged period of flailing that kept Beckett from tolerating any teaching position, from seriously trying to acquire some paying job, or from having a workable relationship with a girlfriend. The bright spot of his early twenties was the exchange lectureship in English he held at École Normale Supérieur in Paris from 1928 to 1930. There he made an important friendship with the previous exchange lecturer Thomas McGreevy (later MacGreevy), who would become his primary confidant for many years. He cemented his friendship with Alfred Péron, who had been an exchange lecturer in French at Beckett's alma mater, Trinity College Dublin. McGreevy introduced Beckett to James Joyce and other members of the Irish literary circle that Beckett joined in Paris. He had found his people, and the place where he felt at home.

During these same years, against his parents' strong disapproval, he had a love relationship with his first cousin, Peggy Sinclair, who lived in Germany with her family. The affair fell apart, perhaps because they were cousins, perhaps because of Beckett's ambivalence about sex and commitment. When he returned to Ireland to take up a two-year position as a lecturer in French at Trinity College Dublin, he suffered so deeply from shyness and dislike of the role he was supposed to play in the classroom that he resigned after a little more than a year. Fleeing back to Paris, he completed *Dream* in 1932. Peggy Sinclair, who had moved on to a new German lover, died of tuberculosis in 1933.

My first encounter with *Dream* did not go well. I was put off by the presentation of Belacqua, who is full of disgust at himself and even more disgust at the sexual hunger of his lover, on whom he bestows a fantasy name, "the Smeraldina-Rima." The opening scene sets up the romantic occasion of a lovers' farewell as the Smeraldina-Rima departs, waving frantically, from a ship returning her to Germany. Belacqua lingers on the Dublin wharf having all the wrong feelings: instead of heartbreak or longing he has to work hard at conjuring up emotion of any kind. The honesty about his difficulty in coughing up the expected feeling is equally a self-accusation: deep down, our hero fears, he is cold of heart. I found myself torn, admiring the refusal of generic sentiment and feeling the prison of Belacqua's self-enclosure.

The story takes him between visits to his lover in Germany and returns to Dublin, where he shares intellectual and spiritual relations free of sex with a woman he calls the Alba. The novel struck me as embarrassingly autobiographical: the Smeraldina-Rima is a grotesquely misogynistic version of Peggy Sinclair, while the idealized Alba is based on Beckett's undergraduate infatuation with Ethna MacCarthy, a brilliant fellow student at Trinity College Dublin. Other women and men in Beckett/Belacqua's life are also turned into cartoons. Belacqua's failure to love any of them, and his sardonic portraits of friends and mentors, all spoke of entrapment in a depression that manifests itself in scorn and superiority. The novel seemed a perfect candidate for the bottom drawer. As he grew beyond these unhappy years, Beckett thought so too.

The story of a young man who breaks off a physical love relationship with the Smeraldina-Rima in favor of an intellectual and spiritual connection with the Alba invokes the form of the *Bildungsroman*. Beckett makes it clear that he has no intention of writing one. Part One, the childhood, covers one-third of a page, where it mocks the notion that a boy's experience forms his character. We are enjoined to "Behold Belacqua an overfed child" running madly after a horse van until he's rewarded by seeing the horse's tail arch for a "gush of mard. Ah…!" The boy is then "to be surprised" later in childhood climbing trees and sliding down a gym rope. These three tiny, distant visions of a physical body speeding through its childhood could be about anyone. Nor will we learn of Smeraldina-Rima's origins, "dull as ditchwater…That tires us. As though the gentle reader could be nothing but an insurance broker or a professional punter. The background pushed up as a guarantee—that tires us."[3] From that pose of weary disillusion, Beckett announces the end of character as the nineteenth century knew it. It can't be explained by relating the circumstances of biography, nor does it lend itself to the conclusions of plot. Belacqua's tale ends in a drunken stupor, without decision or enlightenment.

My engagement with *Dream* quickened when I left the relationships behind and concentrated on the narrator's meditation on the nature of character. In this autobiographical work, the fantastically named characters are caricatures of actual people in Beckett's life. When the narrator steps away from the story, he does everything he can to blur the lines between real people and fictional characters, as if he were pointing surreptitiously at his own practice. His sprightly voice rejects the way characters are schematically constructed by nineteenth-century novelists, while insisting on the difficulty of controlling his own inventions. "The fact of the matter is we do not know quite where we are in this story. It is possible that some of our creatures will do their dope all right and give no trouble. And it is certain that others will not" (*Dream*, 9).

Novelists sometimes talk about how their characters take over and direct their stories during the writing process, without acknowledging as much within the boundaries of their finished products. Beckett wanted to make the uncertainties of composition part of the entertainment. He would continue throughout his work to refer to his characters as creatures. Creatures may be human, but they are part of some larger earthly eco-system, and they are unburdened by the ethical implications of "character." They do not have to be defined by a certain set of physical, mental, or moral characteristics that remain consistent. Creatures may or not "do their dope all right," or they might start to perform in unanticipated ways. Whether or not Beckett can make them "stand for something" remains to be seen. He already knows that the figure he calls Nemo cannot: "it is almost certain that Nemo cannot be made, at least not by us, to stand for anything. *He is simply not that kind of person*" (*Dream*, 9–10).

One of the uncertainties comes through in the anxious repetition of the phrase "stand for." Beckett asks whether fictional characters point to, imitate, or give the illusion of being people who live in a recognizable world. Or do they stand for some idea? Can a writer "make them" perform either possibility? As a reader, I know that characters are just verbal constructions, but I believe in their lives if the novel is successful, and they can become part of the inner repertoire of people I know and speculate about. There is, after all, something natural going on when readers—or later fiction writers—find themselves trying to imagine the further lives of characters, beyond the pages of the novel in which they appear.

The case of Nemo, or "no one," adds to the puzzle. A shady entity who leans over Dublin bridges, and who may or may not die by suicide, Nemo is a second-hand character, borrowed from Dickens's *Bleak House*, where his non-name is a pseudonym that covers over his secret past as the illegitimate heroine's father. No such plot revelation will occur in this story, yet Nemo does hover as if he held some undefinable meaning for Belacqua, who sometimes shares his dark meditations on the bridge, and who refuses to believe the police report that Nemo has committed suicide.

He is simply not that kind of person. That teasing phrase gathers more force when it is later used about Belacqua as well. Trying to wrap my mind around its possibilities, I hear it said aloud, as if someone were defending a friend against some misconstruction. In the fictional context, the narrator is defending one of his characters, Nemo, against a reader who's trying to fit Nemo into some fictional role—perhaps as a portent of death, or a father figure that casts a shadow on Belacqua's future. Amid the array of fantastical names bestowed on the other characters in *Dream*, the designation "Nemo" could say "he is not a caricature, but a person." Or "this character can't stand for anyone or anything; he is unknowable." Or "he has no name because he, unlike the others, is merely an invented entity in a novel." The simple sentence pushes ingeniously at the boundary between real people and fictional characters.

When Beckett later became a playwright, he stuck to the principle that his creatures could not be fully known. Actors learned not to ask him to explain more about a character's feelings or motives so they could get insights about how to perform it. According to Beckett, he knew as little about his characters as they did. They did not stand for anything else. What could be known about them was what was on the page, and the actor's task was to produce the words he had written with the right voicing and rhythm. As he wrote to the German director Carlheinz Caspari about a 1953 production of *Waiting for Godot,*

The characters are living creatures, only just living perhaps, they are not emblems. I can readily understand your unease at their lack of characterization. But I would urge you to see in them less the result of an attempt at abstraction, something I am almost incapable of, than a refusal to tone down all that is at one and the same time complex and amorphous in them.[4]

Beckett links characterization with emblem-making or abstraction. Precisely because they are not firmly delineated, he can imagine his characters as living creatures. What you get on the page is just a fragment of what they are, or might be, in life. If there's a bit of posturing in all this, it's fundamentally a serious questioning of the relationship between made-up characters and living people. Both, Beckett insists, must be granted the gift of being at least partly unknowable. Growing up in a family with no tradition of academic or literary life, he was accustomed to cherishing the privacy of his own thoughts under the assumption that others would not understand them. His defense of his characters' right not to be thoroughly defined or known was, I think, a reflex of his need to protect "what is at the same time complex and amorphous" in himself.

Music is the art form that does not stand for anything beyond its sounds and motions. Throughout *Dream*, Beckett invokes musical forms as metaphors for narrative. But not all forms of music serve as ideals. As part of his critique of character, Beckett offers "a little story about China in order to orchestrate what we mean." He tells a legend of Lîng-Liûn, who discovered that blowing into a notched reed would give forth the sound of his own voice. The art form "liu-liu" is a composition made up of reed flutes, each playing only its six assigned notes within a scheme devised by the master. If Beckett's characters were like that, "we could write a little book that would be purely melodic, think how nice that would be, linear, a lovely Pythagorean chain-chant solo of cause and effect, a one-fingered teleophony that would be a pleasure to hear" (*Dream*, 10). His snarky voice mocks a reader's desire for controlled clarity and simplicity, possible only when a character is given a limited repertoire of identifying traits.

No, single cause-and-effect melodies will not do for creatures. Nemo "is not a note at all but the most regrettable simultaneity of notes" (*Dream*, 11). Only a symphony, not simple melody, would suffice for him. It would follow that character cannot really be told in a novel at all, dependent as it is on one voice speaking at a time. Getting it right would require multiple instruments playing different things at the same time, with harmony, changes of key, disharmony, counterpoint, and all the other musical possibilities. At the end of this meditation the narrator gives up on any attempt to make Belacqua stand for anything definite either. "Indeed, we tend, on second thoughts, to smell the symphonic rat in our principal boy" (*Dream*, 11).

You could argue that the crowded, multi-voiced novels of the nineteenth century were more symphonic than anything Beckett wrote. By way of answer, Beckett invoked his favorite bête-noir, Balzac.

> He is absolute master of his material, he can do what he likes with it, he can foresee and calculate its least vicissitude, he can write the end of the book before he has finished the first paragraph, because he has turned all his creatures into clockwork cabbages and can rely on their staying put wherever needed or staying going at whatever speed in whatever direction he chooses. (*Dream*, 119–20)

Balzac's narrative imperialism is deadly, Beckett insists, like a world under chloroform. The unruliness of *Dream* offers itself as a living organism, full of contradictions and second thoughts. At this stage Beckett still needs to assert his originality by kicking against earlier traditions of storytelling. Still, I honor his impulse to assert the symphonic depth and mystery of character. It gets me thinking about the aspects of people and imagined people that I recognize as "characteristic," and the parts that I will never quite hear, as they play their little counterpoints in the background. Against the painfully self-destructive story of young Belacqua, Beckett's attention to such questions comes as a welcome antidote.

The narrator's parodies of lofty literary styles are further signatures of Beckett's apprentice writing. His voice takes on the mock-regal pronoun "we," and indulges freely in unruly liveliness of mind, sometimes recalling the meta-fictional antics of the eighteenth-century English novelists Sterne and Fielding. The shape-shifting storyteller goes in and out of identifiable literary languages from one moment to the next, puncturing whatever style he's imitating with a thump of earthy diction. It begins with the book's title, which riffs on Tennyson's early poem "A Dream of Fair Women" and the medieval predecessor that prompted Tennyson, Chaucer's "The Legend of Good Women." "Fair to middling," a colloquial expression meaning "average," or "moderately good," brings with it a suggestion of grading quality—in cotton, sheep, or women. Setting itself in line with dream visions that praise a series of legendary women notable for faithfulness or beauty, "fair to middling" brings Beckett's own project abruptly down to ground level.

In one scene Belacqua lies asleep on a tugboat bringing him home to Ireland from a sojourn in Germany. He's momentarily surrounded by shades of classical homecomings: "Thus dusk shall ere long gather about him—unless to be sure we take it into our head to scuttle at dead of night the brave ship where he now lies a-dreaming." The archaic language deflates when we hear that the whole business could be abruptly scuttled if the narrator were so inclined—an early instance of the habitual move in which a Beckett narrator talks out loud about possible directions his narrative could take, only to discard them. But what comes next surprised me:

> L'andar su che porta? ...
> Oh but the bay, Mr. Beckett, didn't you know, about your brow.
>
> (Dream, 141)

The Italian is Dante's, from Belacqua's speech in Canto IV of the Purgatorio: "What is the use of going up?" Beckett seems to be associating Dantean Belacqua's refusal to move toward redemption with the possibility that his modern Belacqua might remain indefinitely afloat in a liminal realm between sea and land. That fantasy is immediately shut down by the voice that sardonically addresses "Mr. Beckett," twitting the real-life novelist for trying to don the laurel wreath that traditionally adorns Dante's brow. Suddenly the author becomes a character in his own fiction.

"Mr. Beckett" gets a return appearance when the illusion of abiding in a fictional world is further disrupted. Now the sardonic voice relaxes into a more playful mood, and Beckett's comic genius begins to show its face. The narrator meets Belacqua in some leisured Viennese afterlife of the present fiction. "Years later," he claims, "in the course of a stroll in the Prater (yes, it was in the Prater, we were strolling in the Prater, we were strolling to the horse-races), he furnished me with the details of this visitation" (Dream, 185). It now appears that the narrator knew his

character "in real life," intimately enough for confidences that supposedly verify the story being told about him. Beckett indulges in
a multi-layered joke that pokes fun at novels that make truth
claims for invented stories, and further blurs the boundaries
between real lives and fictional characters. Then he admits,
"Strictly speaking this Belacqua of later days stands outside the
enceinte of our romaunt" (*Dream*, 186). The archaic French conjures up a medieval verse romance enclosed by a wall of fortifica-
tion. If this were a proper novel, Beckett jokes, it would stay within
the boundaries of acceptable narrative behavior.

But we aren't speaking strictly; right away Mr. Beckett the
author joins his character and narrator onstage. They watch him
and speculate: "Guardedly, reservedly, we beheld him. He was hat-
less, he whistled a scrap of an Irish air, his port and mien were
jaunty resignation." Mr. Beckett is heard referring to himself as
John of the Crossroads, and echoing St. Augustine's most quoted
quip: "Give me chastity" he mentioned, "and continence, only not
yet" (*Dream*, 186). Mr. Beckett as an insouciant man about town
observed from the outside by his own fictive inventions is a
delightful absurdity; you can't help laughing. And it's a little fore-
taste of the mature Beckett's idea that the author, however well
concealed, is an essential actor in his own fictions.

The parody of a generic Irish author as he might appear to random observers in a foreign street carries overtones of Irish
Catholicism, and brings James Joyce to mind. During his pre-war
years in Paris, Beckett was part of Joyce's inner circle, giving
friendship and service in many forms to Joyce and his family.
Dream of Fair to Middling Women, with its wildly erudite and allusive
flights of rhetoric, was quite often described as an imitation of
Joyce, and it surely would not have been written without the

example of Joyce's work. For a while young Beckett became quite a slavish imitator of Joyce's appearance, which may help account for the self-parody as Mr. Beckett. When he did write a truly Joycean passage in *Dream*, however, he bent it to his own purposes. It occurs when Belacqua, dangerously ill, travels to Germany to effect an emergency repair of his relationship with the Smeraldina-Rima and her family. Pages of nightmarish, fragmentary images flicker by to dramatize Belacqua's delirium. Then the narrator dismisses them: "All that sublimen of blatherskite just to give some idea of the state the poor fellow was in on arrival" (*Dream*, 74). His imitation is also a declaration of independence from Joyce's late style. That was as important to him as his resistance to premodern novelists.

In 1933, as *Dream of Fair to Middling Women* came back with one disheartening rejection letter after another, Beckett put together a collection of ten short stories about Belacqua that was published under the title *More Pricks Than Kicks*. To fill out the book, he included two sequences from *Dream*, rescued and revised to fit into the trajectory traced by the other stories. Beginning with Belacqua's antisocial student days, these stories romp through his three marriages, a wedding, death, and funeral arrangements. Belacqua's hapless submission to those worldly protocols ends with his abrupt and meaningless demise from a basic surgical error. The rococo improvisations of *Dream*'s narrator disappear in the condensed form of the short story, but many elements of the novel linger. The narrative is still wedded to Belacqua's point of view. He flees from social and romantic entanglements, while the supporting characters exert themselves to bring him to heel. Courtship, marriage, and death get the slapstick treatment, as their busy arrangers affect conventional emotional attitudes in order to pursue their own love interests.

I will concentrate on just one stand-alone story that revives the question of character. "Ding-Dong" opens with an I-narrator who claims to have been an intimate confidant of Belacqua. His friend's need to analyze and explain himself leads the narrator to complain about his inconsistency.

> In his anxiety to explain himself he was liable to come to grief. Nay, this anxiety in itself, or so at least it seemed to me, constituted a breakdown in the self-sufficiency which he never wearied of arrogating to himself, a sorry collapse of my little internus homo, and alone sufficient to give him away as inept ape of his own shadow. But he wriggled out of everything by pleading that he had been drunk at the time, or that he was an incoherent person and content to remain so, and so on. He was an impossible person in the end. I gave him up in the end because he was not *serious*.[5]

The passage strikes me as an uncanny critique of Beckett's own state at this period. His ability to assess himself as he might appear in the eyes of others is on full display. The self-sufficiency he so desires is undercut by anxiety and neediness; his belief in the incoherence of character is a way out of commitment to anyone or anything. The so-clever insult, "an inept ape of his own shadow," is a depressive accusation of insubstantiality. Yet as the story takes shape, the self-accusation takes a more empathetic turn.

The narrator finds Belacqua impossible because he wriggles out of being serious or consistent. "But notice the double response, like two holes to a burrow," he remarks of his friend (*More Pricks Than Kicks*, 42). It's the image of a creature that will construct an emergency exit in case of invasion by others. The story turns out to be about Belacqua's helpless entrapment by a huckster woman who accosts him in a pub, fascinates him, and shames him into buying tickets for a seat in heaven. I can feel his terrible sense of being skewered by his own kindness, and his embarrassing exposure in front of the workers drinking around him. The "ding-dong" Belacqua who veers from one extreme to the other is finally captured in a humiliating scene that brings him into sympathetic focus. The intellectual self-consciousness that allows Beckett to render himself from the outside has been transformed into the emotional self-consciousness of public embarrassment.

Beckett's active resistance to standard life patterns and predictable emotions was not only an adolescent rebellion but a lifelong tendency. His letters sometimes express his dismay with astonishing directness. After his father died in 1933, he confided in his aunt Cissie Sinclair about a period of stress with his widowed mother, amid preparations for his brother Frank's wedding.

> All the presents pouring in, a gong this morning so terrible, the impediments of detached domesticities, the circle closing round... To be welded together with gongs and tea-trolleys, the bars against the sky, how hopeless. Is that what "home" means for all women, solid furniture and not to be overlooked, or is there another sense of home in some of them, or are there some who don't want a home, who have had enough of that?[6]

He's yearning for a woman who would share his horror of bourgeois domesticity. Two months later, Beckett wrote more vehemently to his confidant Thomas McGreevy about his mother:

> As it has been all this time, she wanting me to behave in a way agreeable to her in her October of alphabetic gentility, or to her friends ditto, or to the business code of my father idealized— dehumanized...the grotesque can go no further. It is a little like after a long forenoon of thumb screws being commanded by the

bourreau [the executioner] to play his favorite song without words with feeling.   (*Letters*, 1:552)

May Beckett's display of genteel mourning offended Beckett deeply. She and her husband had led rather separate lives before his death; now, according to her son, she hypocritically dramatized her grief and reduced Bill's life to an ideal. The pressure to join her sentimental song was a form of torture to him. The outburst captures the love, rage, and bitterness that bound mother and son. The fact that he still relied on her for money was another painful twist in the knot.

Those who tried to lure him out of depressiveness also had to be fended off. In *Dream of Fair to Middling Women* Belacqua's own family is barely there except in the calm phrase "the blue eyes of home" and a few mentions of a brother and father. For just an instant, though, "Mother" intrudes as Belacqua departs for Germany to see the Smeraldina-Rima: "His Mother put her head into the taxi and before she broke down (the Mother, not the taxi) breathed 'be happy' as if to insinuate: 'again and again I request you to be merry'" (*Dream*, 12).

In 1960, as Beckett's intimacy with BBC producer and critic Barbara Bray was beginning, we can hear a recurrence of the old anger. Bray was thinking of moving from London to Paris, and Beckett had made it clear that his commitment to Suzanne Deschevaux-Dumesnil could not be abandoned. He would be with Bray as much as he could, but he would not tell anyone how to behave, and he scorned the notion that she or anyone else could arrange for his happiness.

We go round in the same old circles always, and it is tiring. If it is a trickle of sad phrases it is because I am sad and tired and coming to an end and don't talk to me for God's sake about the duty of happiness, do you want me to put on a black moustache and pad out my cheeks with cotton wool, I'll be very glad if you come over and do all I can and enjoy doing it to give you at least a little of what you want. But it's not much I can do and there's not much I can say.[7]

In 1934–35, Beckett was living in London and undergoing psychoanalysis with W.R. Bion for the acute depression, insomnia, wild heartbeat, and panic attacks that had worsened after his father's death. Though he had to depend on May Beckett to pay for the therapy, he was able to commit himself fully to its course, while reading widely in psychoanalytic theory. The perspective he achieved, writes biographer James Knowlson, "offers perhaps the first convincing explanation of how the arrogant, disturbed, narcissistic young man of the early 1930s could possibly have evolved into someone who was noted later for his extraordinary kindness, courtesy, concern, generosity, and almost saintly 'good works.'"[8]

The evolution Knowlson mentions begins to show itself as early as 1935, when Beckett began a new novel, Murphy. It was designed to be a book that might—and finally did—behave itself well enough to get published. The performative excesses of Dream disappear from its short, punchy sentences. Beckett's hostility to previous novel conventions disappears, and he begins to make good-natured use of them. The book reads as a comedy, though it gathers other tones as it goes along. The Belacqua connection shows up briefly as Murphy's favorite escape fantasy, which "belonged to those that lay just beyond the frontiers of suffering; it was the first landscape of freedom."[9] The place of freedom that Murphy seeks is now reimagined as freedom from human suffering. Like freedom from social conventions, it is impossible to achieve. In this book, however, the narrator maintains some distance from Murphy's self-isolating tendencies, and brings him closer to the rest of the human race.

Murphy has invented a practical household technique to rid himself of the burdens of having a defined character in the world: he binds his naked self with scarves into a rocking chair and rocks madly until he reaches a blissful state of oblivion. This masturbatory practice gives way to an actual love affair. When the rocker overturns, leaving him pathetically trapped underneath, he is fortuitously rescued by our heroine Celia, a descendent of fictional prostitutes who turn out to have hearts of gold. The two begin to share Murphy's room, and to engage in a push-pull dialogue as each attempts to bend the other to his or her idea of life. This time Celia's point of view is given equal credence. In part, however, the story becomes a morality tale about what happens to love when a woman tells her beloved to live as she sees fit.

Murphy battles with Celia over that question, insisting with unusual passion that if she loved him she could not want him to change. Celia insists that she will leave if Murphy does not get a job so she can leave her life as a prostitute; Murphy protests that she is negating the very being she fell in love with. He finally gives in to a job search, though he spends most of his time loitering in London parks, encountering odd urban figures, and waiting for the end of the day so he can go home. Through one of his chance encounters he stumbles on a live-in job as an orderly in a mental asylum, and dies in a freak accident there.

While Murphy is absent, Celia morphs into a Murphy-like state, spending hours doing nothing, rocking in his rocker and waiting anxiously for him. She begins to understand his sense of life, and to love him truly as she loses him. In an unusual turn to judgment, the narrator chastens:

When [Love's] end had been Murphy transfigured and transformed, happily caught up in some salaried routine, means had not been lacking. Now that its end was Murphy at any price, in whatsoever shape or form, so long as he was lovable, i.e. present in person, means were lacking, as Murphy had warned her they would be. Women are really extraordinary, the way they want to give their cake to the cat and have it. They never quite kill the thing they think they love, lest their instinct for artificial respiration should go abegging. (*Murphy*, 202–3)

The outburst of bitter misogyny in the last two sentences stands out from the usual tones in *Murphy*. It's a throw-back, more relevant to Beckett's general suspicion of women—his mother in particular—than to Celia, who does come to understand her man and her mistake. After reading Beckett's earlier female portraits, I was glad of Celia and her bedridden grandfather Mr. Willoughby Kelly, who bring a dimension of affectionate humanity into the novel.

Murphy kept reminding me of early Dickens. It is Beckett's London novel, conscious of nineteenth-century predecessors like Dickens and George Gissing, whose intimate knowledge of London streets was realized in their characters' precise walking routes through particular areas of the city. Beckett, too, spent a good deal of his lonely time in London walking the streets and haunting the parks of the city. Like Dickens, he makes use of the city as a place of chance encounter, populating it with comic portraits of eccentric urban figures.

In chapter 2, Celia tells her grandfather the story of her new relationship with Murphy. She begins with the details of the way they met in the street, while the narrator presents himself as the editor of her speech: "Celia's account, expurgated, accelerated, improved and reduced, of how she came to speak of Murphy, gives the following" (*Murphy*, 12). The pretense that there's a real London dialect lurking behind the words on the page carries on Beckett's teasing habit of positing a "real" person that hides somewhere behind the fiction.

Mr. Kelly proves to be a reader who's initially resistant to her step-by-step mode of narration. Instead of hearing exactly where and how the lovers met, he wants to know about Murphy's character. After Celia describes their first encounter at a precise intersection of Chelsea roads, he protests: "'But I beseech you,' said Mr. Kelly, 'be less beastly circumstantial. The junction for example of Edith Grove, Cremorne Road and Stadium Street, is indifferent to me. Get up to your man'" (*Murphy*, 13). When she persists, Mr. Kelly protests again: "Hell roast this story." He doesn't want a Dickensian street encounter. Like a disapproving patriarch, he wants to know who Murphy is: "What is he? Where does he come from? What is his family? What does he do? Has he any money? Has he any prospects? Has he any retrospects? Is he, has he, anything at all?"

"Has he any retrospects?"—that little swerve charms me every time. Celia is unable to give a satisfactory answer to any of Mr. Kelly's questions. There's no past and no future: "Murphy was Murphy" (*Murphy*, 17). As Celia's story winds on, her grandfather, like any attentive reader, becomes engaged in its details. His emotional responses to each part of the story fly in every direction. He can sympathize with Murphy's point of view at one moment, and in another order Celia to leave him; yet he knows that passion will have its day. As she departs, he wants nothing to do with the mess she has gotten herself into, and the two seem to separate for good. "Now I have no one, thought Celia, except possibly Murphy" (*Murphy*, 25). Other characters will repeat variations of that formula. "Now I have no one, except possibly x," they think, or "Now I have no one, not even y." The human suffering in *Murphy* gradually comes into view as a problem of isolation.

Beckett's interest in mental illness during his London years led him into a Dickens-like piece of social research. With the help of his physician friend Geoffrey Thompson, he paid several visits to "Bedlam," the Bethlem Royal Hospital for mental patients, becoming acquainted with a variety of illnesses that he made use of when Murphy takes his job in a similar institution. I can imagine Beckett sympathetically observing those who lived in conditions of self-enclosure far more extreme and untreatable than his own.

Loneliness—the other side of the instinct to avoid other humans—lies close to the surface of the novel. Murphy wants to love, and yearns to find the solace of understanding in one other being. When he goes to his job at the mental asylum, he believes he might find that mutual recognition in the schizophrenic patient Mr. Endon, with whom he plays hopelessly inconclusive games of chess. His disillusionment and death follow when he realizes the futility of that desire for connection. Mr. Endon is incapable of recognizing his chess partner as another human. Murphy flees, sheds his hospital clothes, and tries to summon an image of anyone he has known, without success. "He could not get a picture in his mind of any creature he had met, animal or human" (*Murphy*, 251–2). Even in his imagination, the world of creatures—the world Beckett summons to keep out the void—has been utterly blanked out. That ultimate mental isolation is effectively his end. He tries to calm himself by rocking in his chair, and is—offstage—killed by an explosion in the jerry-rigged gas apparatus he has hooked up to keep him warm in his attic retreat.

A mechanical kind of loneliness also figures in the novel's other plot, in which an ensemble of pompous and conniving academic Dubliners and their cadre of lady loves make plans to go after Murphy and bring him back into their fold. They appear in carefully dated alternating chapters, again akin to Dickens's bad-guy gangs that plot to hunt down and disrupt the fortunes of the heroes and heroines. In Beckett's case, their deceptively polite machinations arise from a terror of isolation; each is desperate to snag a desirable partner by betraying and manipulating the others. Their desires click on and off as they play an increasingly crass game of sexual musical chairs. Traveling to London to find Murphy, they move in with Celia, who wants only to be reunited with her lover. By the time they find Murphy he is dead. The final chapters make grotesque comedy of the group's antics at the postmortem and their heartlessly random disposal of his ashes.

"All the puppets in this book whinge sooner or later, except Murphy, who is not a puppet," the narrator declares (122). If *Dream of Fair to Middling Women* wondered whether its unruly characters would behave properly, *Murphy*'s Dublin characters play the roles assigned to them, like puppets on strings. Murphy—and, I would add, Celia and her grandfather—is endowed with more sympathetic depths. When Thomas McGreevy praised the manuscript of the novel, Beckett described his desire to play down the death of his hero, along with his sense of partial failure.

> I chose this because it seemed to me to consist better with the treatment of Murphy throughout, with the mixture of compassion, patience, mockery, and "tat twam asi" that I seem to have directed on him throughout, with the sympathy going so far and no further (then losing patience) as in the short statement of his mind's fantasy of himself. There seemed to me always the risk of taking him

too seriously and separating him too sharply from the others. As it is I do not think the mistake (Aliosha mistake) has been altogether avoided. (*Letters*, 1:350)

The letter offers a glimpse into Beckett's clear sense of artistic design in the new novel. "Tat twam asi," a Sanskrit term, was familiar to Beckett and McGreevy via Schopenhauer, for whom it signified "this other is thyself" (*Letters*, 1:353n.). Always his own best critic, Beckett admits that he identified with his hero more fully than he had intended. His sly ambition peeks out when he aligns his mistake with Dostoevsky's account of Aliosha in *The Brothers Karamazov*.

Murphy's aspirations to freedom, his wind-tossed modes of being, and his crashing end are movingly figured in a sequence of metaphorical scenes about kite-flying. As he was beginning to compose the novel in September 1935, Beckett wrote to McGreevy about his fascination with old men flying kites at the Round Pond in Kensington. He admired the care with which the kites were fashioned and prepared for transport in separate parts, the tension of the launch into the wind, and the subtle technique of keeping the kites in the air, even as they fly out of sight.

> I was really rooted to the spot yesterday, unable to go away and wondering what was keeping me. Extraordinary effect too of birds flying close to the kites but beneath them. My next old man, or old young man, not of the big world, but of the little world, must be a kite-flyer. (*Letters*, 1:274)

As Beckett muses on, kite-flying becomes "disinterested, like a poem." I like to imagine him recalling the kite flown by damaged Mr. Dick in Dickens's *David Copperfield*, who lightens his heart by sending his troubles sky-high. Beckett's kite-flyers extend

Murphy's romantic flights to other characters who cherish the ecstasies of wind-borne escape, and accept the inevitable descent to earth.

Grandfather Kelly, confined to bed or wheelchair, is still handy with the construction and launching of kites. In an early fantasy he sees himself as both flyer and kite: "Already in position, straining his eyes for the speck that was he, digging in his heels against the immense pull skyward" (*Murphy*, 25). He is not so different from Murphy after all. Later, Celia observes the kites of other flyers:

> Only two rose steadily, a tandem, coupled abreast like the happy tug and barge, flown by the child from a double winch. She could just discern them, side by side high above the trees, specks against the east darkening already. The wrack broke behind them as she watched, for a moment they stood out motionless and black, in a glade of limpid viridescent sky. (*Murphy*, 152)

The lovely lyricism gently figures both Murphy's desire to soar beyond sight and the "tandem" love between him and Celia, becoming static and moribund as it is extinguished by darkness. In the novel's valedictory scene Mr. Kelly flies his own kite.

> Except for the sagging soar of line, undoubtedly superb so far as it went, there was nothing to be seen, for the kite had disappeared from view. Mr. Kelly was enraptured.
>
> ...He fixed with his eagle eye a point in the empty sky where he fancied the kite to swim into view, and wound carefully in.
>
> (*Murphy*, 280)

The echoes of Keats's sonnet "On First Looking into Chapman's Homer" underline the rapture of revelation and discovery. Celia can't participate; she has lost Murphy and now observes the kites without joy. She catches her grandfather dozing, unable to complete the ritual. He loses hold of the winch; the string snaps. Like the downed kite, he collapses and folds in on himself. The novel ends as Celia pushes him out of the shut-down park: flights of fancy have bowed to the weight of dutiful care. The kite episodes link Murphy's idiosyncratic pursuit of freedom with those of ordinary folk, old men and children, who play out similar yearnings through the art of kite-flying. The sad figure of Celia pushing her comatose grandfather in his wheelchair ends the novel with a sense of genuine loss and loneliness.

Beckett's three pre-war fictions set their romantically flailing protagonists against deeply sardonic portraits of the social worlds they are attempting to defy, putting his own prolonged adolescent anguish on display. Only his later fame made it inevitable that these works would sooner or later be rescued from obscurity and brought back to light. Their lasting fascination, for me, remains in the connection between his long, guilty effort to pull away from his family's social expectations and his precocious refusal of the expectations raised by the novel form itself. While he was still in the Irish context, he vented his sarcasm, his erudition, and his frustration in fiction that paraded his powers of scorn and rejection, and then grew to accommodate an easier playfulness, and a keener sadness. His ability to invent new voices each time he began a new work was already apparent. He knew from the start that he wanted to treat character more radically than he was yet able to accomplish. After *Murphy*, Beckett would abandon the love plot that had always been a primary structuring principle of novels. He would gradually pull his creatures away from realistic contexts altogether, allowing them to encounter others mainly in solitary acts of reminiscence or invention. He would try to get at the rhythm—and the comedy—of human minds pulled this way and that, as they talk themselves through the days of their lives.

In 1939, now permanently settled in Paris, Beckett and his close friend Alfred Péron set about translating *Murphy* into French. The translation would not come out until after the war, when it garnered as little attention as the English version of 1938. By that time Péron, who had originally led Beckett into underground resistance work, had suffered the fate of Jews and resisters at the hands of the Gestapo. Arrested in 1942, he was deported to a concentration camp in 1943, and died in transit back to France on April 30, 1945, the day of Hitler's suicide. Beckett remained close to Péron's widow, Mania, who often checked his proofs for him. On April 29, 1951, a day before the anniversary of Péron's death, he responded to Mania's question about Murphy: "I don't think Murphy could have committed suicide, in the material circumstances, but the possibility can't be ruled out. In any case he was already dead, as a result of mental suicide. Such is my humble opinion" (*Letters*, 2:247).

"Mental suicide," as *Murphy* defines it, would be the death of the imagination. By 1951 Beckett had completed his novel trilogy, which sometimes blurred the line between the end of life and literal death. In this note to Mania, the phrase might also make an oblique reference to Alfred Péron: what would his mind have become after the horrors of the concentration camp? More directly it refers to Murphy's end, when, unable to recall any living being, he gives up on his last hope of connection. As a comment on character, though, the answer is classic Beckett. What he knew, or could know, about Murphy was confined to the words he had written on paper years before. The possibility that Murphy had a life of his own that his author couldn't fathom hovers in the air, just out of reach.

FIRST-PERSON SINGULAR

But bear in mind that I who hardly ever talk about myself talk
about little else.
                                  —Samuel Beckett to Georges Duthuit, March 9, 1949

When I returned to the opening pages of *Molloy*, I found
myself in awe. Here it is at last, I thought, the authentic
voice of doubt. Molloy is in his mother's room, but he doesn't
know how he has come there, or why he is writing the pages he's
told to write by an unidentified "they." He's not sure whether his
mother is still alive or dead enough to have been buried, but he
seems to have taken her place. He doesn't believe he has the brain
power left to write. Then his writerly imagination turns to the retrospective tale of his recent past. It begins as Molloy, from a Belacqua-
like post high on a grey rock, watches intently as two distant figures
he calls A and C walk out of the town and return. Molloy fills them
with feelings, speculation, and projections of his own fears and anxieties. They rise into view and fall out of sight; Molloy sees the pair
coming face to face in a trough that he couldn't have seen from his
perch. Or perhaps the hills are imaginary and the land is perfectly
flat. It is all told sweetly and patiently, with a feeling of acceptance
that replaces the scornful edginess in Beckett's earlier work.[1]

It's tempting to think that Beckett has suddenly, at 41, come
into his true voice. His turn to composing in French first-person

narrative seems to have released the full force of his originality. But there's a path to trace before his arrival in *Molloy*, and it leads through the war, the immediate postwar period, and the stories Beckett wrote in 1946. The homeless wanderers and wasting old men who populate the works of 1946–50 have known better days, but they know those days will not return, that their only future is the death that never quite arrives. In their singularity they carry, lightly enough, the specter of Europe's orphaned millions in motion, fleeing countries, sheltering anywhere, losing limbs, losing minds, expelled from native places, incarcerated in concentration camps or military hospitals, and let go, with nowhere to go.

Samuel Beckett and Suzanne Deschevaux-Dumesnil were among those who fled without knowing where to go.[2] When Beckett's underground resistance cell was exposed in 1942, they took to the road for the south of France, in flight from the Gestapo. Vichy seemed safer than Paris at first; then it wasn't. With the help of this friend and that, walking hours a day, sometimes taking trains, and sleeping wherever they could, they arrived after six weeks in the village of Roussillon, which had somehow escaped German occupation. Beckett did hard labor at a neighboring farm in exchange for food. Suzanne taught piano to some children, using a color method she had developed. In 1945 they returned to their tiny Paris apartment. It would be years before the city's food supply was adequate; it seemed that wartime conditions would never end. Suzanne worked as a dressmaker and scrounged for food wherever she could arrange it.

Beckett had not seen his Irish family for six years. In 1945 he returned to his mother's house to find her shockingly frail. At 74, she had begun the deteriorating process brought on by Parkinson's disease. That cruel condition gradually strips away every physical and mental capacity that had constituted the being, and the dignity, of its victims. Until her death in 1950, Beckett's annual visits home would be confrontations with the relentless decline of May Beckett. Seeing her only at intervals would have made the shock of each stage more vivid.

It may have been her condition in 1945, along with Beckett's wartime experiences, that led to a private recognition of his mission as a writer. This "revelation" has become famous in Beckett lore because it is reinvented in *Krapp's Last Tape* as a vision that took place "at the end of a jetty, in the howling wind, never to be forgotten."[3] Beckett's biographer James Knowlson toned the story down after interviewing his subject during the last months of his life. It took place in his mother's room, Beckett said, where "Molloy and the others came to me the day I became aware of my own folly. Only then did I begin to write the things I feel."[4] Trying to imagine what the content of the insight might have been, I find myself wondering whether Beckett recognized a new literary potential in writing about the ongoing inner life of characters who decline into the infirmity of extreme old age. Their increasing distance from social relationships, home, or work would allow him to concentrate on the thinking and feeling that gets solitary creatures through their remaining portions of life. Writing what he felt in these postwar days would take Beckett into a newly compassionate rendering of his narrators' thoughts, which contrive to make much of what little remains.

The Irish Free State, not yet the Republic of Ireland, had kept itself neutral during the war. That led to difficulties for Beckett in 1945. A person who carried an Irish passport and claimed to have lived in France through the war aroused suspicion at border control on both sides of the Channel. When he tried to make arrangements for his return to Paris, he found that the French border would likely be closed to him, and that he could not keep his Paris apartment, where Suzanne was waiting. The solution was offered by a physician friend, Dr. Alan Thompson, who was part of an Irish Red Cross mission to set up a hospital in Normandy at St.-Lô. Beckett was hired to manage the new hospital's supply chain and to interpret between Irish staff and French workers and patients. From August through December 1945, he worked amid the mud and rubble of a town destroyed by Allied bombing, as the hospital gradually took shape. He was doing inventories, translating, and driving—despite his bad eyesight—through all manner of bad weather. James Knowlson is eloquent on the subject of St.-Lô and its influence on Beckett's vision:

> It was in St.-Lô that he witnessed real devastation and misery: buildings—each one someone's home—reduced to rubble; possessions blown to pieces; a ward full of patients ill with tuberculosis...people in desperate need of food and clothing, yet clinging, desperately, to life; a hospital created out of nothing on fields that became churned into a sea of mud.[5]

That international relief work allowed Beckett to stay in France, and to keep his apartment at 6 rue des Favorites. It was also an intimate encounter with postwar suffering.

The writing began soon after he returned to Paris, with a set of long stories that all begin with a narrator's eviction from a sheltered situation, leaving him to fend for himself as he can.

Here Beckett made his crucial turn, to first-person retrospective narrative and—after an initial start in English—to French prose. French was now the language of his daily life, and his wartime services had welded him further to his adopted country. The story first titled "Suite" opens as the narrator is ejected from some charitable institution or hospital. Though he tries everything he can think of to persuade the staff to keep him there, he is forced out, wearing ill-fitting old clothes that had belonged to someone else and carrying a small amount of money "to get me started. When it was gone I would have to get more, if I wanted to go on."[6] The French word "suite," meaning continuation or sequence, refers to how he does, and doesn't, go on. It charts the narrator's steps as he weans himself from the powerful urge to be sheltered and cared for in one spot.

The city he knew has changed completely, presumably from unspecified war bombings, though we're left to think the change may also lie in the narrator's altered state of perception. He finds a basement lodging with a landlady who will accept the bizarre spectacle of his outward appearance, but eventually he is rooked out of his remaining money and ejected again. A generous old friend offers him shelter in a cave by the sea, then in a shack in the woods, but he gets more and more unwilling to allow anyone to help him, and he loses his ability to simulate the human gestures that might appeal to other people. He fashions a wooden sandwich board to help him beg in the streets, and finally makes himself a shelter in an abandoned old rowboat, where, leaning against a sack he's filled with grass, he prepares to die. As the end comes crashing upon him, "The memory came faint and cold of the story I might have told, a story in the likeness of my life, I mean without the courage to end or the strength to go on" (*Stories and Texts for Nothing*, 72). *In the likeness of my life*: not autobiography but something emotionally akin to it, as a modern painted portrait distorts and interprets its subject. It's an oblique description of the stories that, Beckett already knows, will follow.

The narrative is stripped down to declarative statements in relatively short sentences. It becomes more lyrically expressive as the narrator loses contact with other human beings, as if the maneuvers of social negotiation had been replaced by a greater openness to the non-human world. In its first published form, however, "Suite" did not have its second half. Beckett submitted the first half to Simone de Beauvoir for the review *Les Temps Modernes*, assuming, without saying so, that the long story would require publication in two parts. After the first was in print, he sent the second part, which de Beauvoir rejected outright. Beckett wrote a letter of protest, which began politely enough: "You have in mind the reputation of your review. That is natural. I am thinking of the character in 'Suite,' denied his rest. That too is natural, I think."[7] His insistence on what is natural may also touch on the pissing, farting, masturbating, and scratching that show up in the narrator's story of his physical decline. Beckett was all too familiar with editorial reactions to his frankness about bodily truths that are rarely spoken.

The letter soon turned into what he might have called a howl: "You are giving me the chance to speak only to retract it before the words have had time to mean anything. You are immobilizing an existence at the very moment at which it is about to take its definitive form. There is something nightmarish about that" (*Letters*, 2:42). Defending the integrity of his work, Beckett insists that its life depends on the shape and movement of the whole. What's "nightmarish" is not the destitution of his character, but cutting off the story's breath before it has arrived at its resting place. When I read the letter, it confirmed something I had absorbed in the course of considering Beckett's works. Though it's easy to get lost in the intricate weeds of whatever section I'm reading, the sense of meaning—I use that word with caution—emerges when I can imagine the overall curve of the narrative, as it rings its changes from beginning to end. That is why my reading of the novels in Beckett's trilogy will try to follow the curve, while stopping to savor some of the small spots that call out for special attention along the way.

Beckett's *cri de coeur* in the Beauvoir letter was about more than the story called "Suite." His own writerly existence was at stake, at the very moment when it was about to take its definitive form.[8] But first, he had one more go at a third-person narrative. *Mercier and Camier*, the odd French novella written after "Suite," clings to an external speaker who introduces himself in the opening sentence: "The journey of Mercier and Camier is one I can tell, if I will, for I was with them all the time."[9] Near the end, however, the two clown characters express discomfort about this extraneous narrator-figure in a dialogue I find especially endearing.

Strange impression, said Mercier, strange impression sometimes
    that we are not alone. You not?
I am not sure I understand, said Camier.
Now quick, now slow, that is Camier all over.
Like the presence of a third party, said Mercier. Enveloping us.
    I have felt it from the start. And I am anything but psychic.
Does it bother you? said Camier.
At first no, said Mercier.
And now? said Camier.
It begins to bother me a little, said Mercier. (*Mercier and Camier*,
    79–80)

The "third party" evokes the fantasy of an invisible being who walks beside us, whether as Christ-figure, external narrator, or wishfully projected protector. Mercier calls it "enveloping," sensing the control of a narrative that surrounds the two of them. In the trilogy Beckett's third-party narrator will disappear, merged with the first-person musings of his narrator-protagonists. Mercier and Camier will be liberated from narration altogether when they are transformed into Vladimir and Estragon, who will come onstage three years later in *Waiting for Godot*.

Beckett's great trilogy was composed between 1947 and 1950, with a short break for *Waiting for Godot* after *Malone Dies*. In the same years May Beckett was slowly disintegrating in Ireland. Whatever the actual content of Beckett's 1945 "revelation" in his mother's room might have been, it took shape in these novels as a colloquy with death: not the medically pronounced end itself, but the long twilight of dying-in-life. He knew that humans inhabit the outskirts of life once they had been stripped of whatever they recognized as themselves. He also knew how valiantly they carry on, as his narrators do, always managing to write or mutter something that attests to an undying consciousness, and contriving new habits to accommodate each new physical disability as it occurs.

These subjects would be merely depressing, were it not for what I'm calling Beckett's voice of doubt. Doubt in this sense is not the opposite of faith, but rather the self-revising, self-correcting flow of colloquial speech that inextricably mixes comedy and pathos. Riding its waves, I laugh and cry at the same time, knowing that Beckett has somehow managed to sketch some of the gestures of my own silent, mundane doubts and worries, and knowing, too, that painful passages of life shake out laughter along with their tears. The difficulty is to describe how Beckett does it. Trying to generalize or categorize his effects is to smother them. Just hearing or reading a passage aloud and trusting the listener to respond in kind is the best way. But I will try to illustrate by pointing to some random examples in *Molloy*. If the overall narrative arc can be charted as a striving soul dispersed in gradual decline, each little section takes off and lands in its own linguistic arena.

Take, for instance, Molloy locked into a room in Lousse's house, where he watches in wonder as the moon passes from one barred window segment to another. Is the moon moving, or is it the room?—"from left to right, but the room not so fast as the moon, or from right to left but the moon not so fast as the room. But can one speak of right and left in such circumstances?" Such attempts at systematic logic inevitably collapse, here replaced by a suddenly romantic image of "that vast yellow light sailing slowly behind my bars" in "its tranquil course." Hearing himself talk, Molloy takes another turn: "How difficult it is to speak of the moon and not lose one's head, the witless moon" (M, 34–5). The long tradition of romantic mooniness thus handily dismissed, he wanders on to other thoughts.

In another vein altogether, Molloy describes a previous relationship with a woman who may have been called Ruth, or perhaps it was Edith. Taken at face value, it's a grotesque account of an ancient crone who leans over the back of a couch to be entered from behind, and pays Molloy for his toil and attention. In the telling it's extremely funny and even oddly tender, as Molloy describes the physical mechanics of the act and worries about whether their activities represent true love—if not, his life would have been devoid of that experience. And why did he not care when she died? And was she really a man or a woman? For purposes of this comedic riff, Molloy's puzzlements are staged in a voice of mock naiveté about sex.

At later stages Molloy's narrative is more fully taken up with attempts to describe in hyper-logical detail how he manages to go forward once his second leg goes as stiff as his first. He painstakingly attempts to explain to his reader which of the two legs he's talking about, or how uneven ground could help him deal with their different lengths. Obsessive attention to each new medical problem as it occurs is surely a shared human experience, which Beckett makes both painful and funny by imitating and exaggerating its contours. He was no stranger to the coming and going of vexing physical symptoms, which he had suffered and endured since childhood.

In another more literary moment, Molloy gets tangled up in Beckett's skepticism about language that falsely clarifies a state of mind. Speaking of a sentence he's just written, he comments "Oh I did not say it in such limpid language. And when I say I said, etc., all I mean is that I knew confusedly things were so, without knowing exactly what it was all about." I'm not sure there's a better description of retrospective telling. When he comes up with fine phrases, Molloy continues, "I am merely complying with the convention that demands you either lie or hold your peace" (M, 82). While both Molloy and Moran cast occasional doubts on the accuracy of their narratives, this instance gets at something slightly different and familiar. Even if there's evidence to the contrary, I sometimes have the feeling that I've stumbled through past episodes in my life in a state of foggy confusion. If I were to describe such moments in words, the fogginess would disappear in the deceptive clarity of retrospective sentences.

If Molloy's narrative has a plot, it concerns his determination to visit his mother, all of the byways and obstacles that prevent him from getting there, and his collapse into a ditch before he reaches his goal. The novel's first pages were composed while Beckett was visiting his mother in 1947. He had always found his visits painful, and often wrote to his confidants about feeling entrapped, frustrated, and physically ill at home. His dislike of Irish provincial culture underlined the sense of duty that propelled him to spend a month each summer in Ireland, while May Beckett lived. After she fell victim to parkinsonism, his letters express more pity for her gradual descent into fragility and dementia. In her increasing neediness, and despite her denial of it, he could at least be of help to her while he was there.

Molloy expresses a version of this emotional complex in the repeated renewals of his need to find his mother and "settle the matter" between them (M, 59). His first resolution comes early on, as a sudden resolution to "go and see that woman" (M, 11). The resolution fades several times along the way. It recurs periodically, however, as his mother's "image, blunted for some time past, was beginning now to harrow me again" (M, 70). Nearing the end of his journey, Molloy begins to fear it's too late, and meditates on his imperative at some length:

> And of myself, all my life, I think I had been going to my mother, with the purpose of establishing our relations on a less precarious footing. And when I was with her, and I often succeeded, I left her without having done anything. And when I was no longer with her I was again on my way to her, hoping to do better next time.   (M, 81)

In the novel's prelude, he finds himself mysteriously transported to his mother's room, where he apparently takes her place in the cycle of dying life.

When I revisited *Molloy* with Beckett's history in mind, I was surprised to find in it a searching encounter with his experience of May Beckett's parenting and decline. When I was younger, I had seen Molloy's attempts to communicate with his mother through a system of knocks on the head as half-cruel and half-comic. I'd read Moran's methods of manipulating his son as a sign of his despicable, hyper-controlling, and suspicious nature. Now my recent experiences with my husband's illness changed my responses to those passages. The half-comic tone in *Molloy* captures the painful helplessness of those who attempt to get through to a person ill with dementia, whose brain has become incapable of learning or remembering anything as apparently simple as a code with four components. The pains Molloy takes to train his mother in a code of communication suggest an odd kind of dedication, its humor sharpened by his need to extract money during his visits. There's even a sly attempt at balance: "I give her credit, though she is my mother, for what she tried to do for me" (M, 14). And perhaps a declaration of something like love, though that's not a word Beckett can even approach without doubting it: "and with her alone, I—no, I can't say it. That is to say I could say it but I won't say it, yes, I could say it easily, because it wouldn't be true" (M, 15). The moment a feeling passes into words they betray the internal truth of the feeling.

Beckett takes on yet heavier territory when he imagines the gap between Moran's relentless critique of his son and the inward fluctuation of his feelings as they veer between distrust and sentimental craving for the son's affection. The sheer mental energy Moran expends in spying on his son and trying to control what he might be doing or thinking shows that the parental relationship is a torment for both parties. At one juncture Moran wishes to tie his son to him by means of a chain, though he knows this to be impossible: what would people think? He knows his son is intelligent, but interrogates him as though he were an idiot, trying to force arbitrary rules into his head. Though he regrets his harshness and expresses love when his son is absent, he does not act on his regrets.

In response, the younger Jacques appears unreadable. He throws a fit here and there, and—not unlike the young Beckett—complains frequently of not feeling well, presumably in hope of getting some kinder attention. For the most part he obeys his father, after putting up some resistance. As Moran's physical condition worsens, he becomes more and more dependent on young Jacques to transport him in the carrier of a bicycle, to buy food, and to build shelters for the night. By the end, he is able to say to the reader that he could not have gotten to Molloy territory without his son. But the son has reached his limit; after a last fight, he abandons his father. The two parent-child stories in *Molloy* are as close as Beckett came to articulating some version of the knotted dynamic between himself and his mother.

The beauty of Molloy's initial meditation on the figures A and C comes into its full intensity only after a reader has completed both Molloy's and Moran's sections. In five packed pages, we watch the writer gradually imagine his way into his new fictional region. The account begins as an apparently simple observation of two separate figures who walk out of the town and then go back on their separate ways, perhaps meeting once, perhaps not. Then the narrator's imagination merges with C, as each of them, character and narrator, embarks on a journey of walking or writing:

> for he went with uncertain step and often stopped to look about him, like someone trying to fix landmarks in his mind, for one day perhaps he may have to retrace his steps, you never know. The treacherous hills where fearfully he ventured were no doubt only known to him from afar.   (M, 5)

I tear myself away with difficulty from quoting the whole page. Summary will not do justice to the fluidity and compassion of such writing, as it begins to veer toward complete identification and sorrow.

> He looks old and it is a sorry sight to see him solitary after so many years, so many days and nights unthinkingly given to that rumour rising at birth and even earlier, What shall I do? What shall I do? now low, a murmur, now precise as a headwaiter's And to follow? and often rising to a scream.   (M, 6)

Who but Beckett could distinguish three distinct levels of existential angst and imagine the middle one as a formal headwaiter waiting for an undecided diner to make a choice? The void that lurks in not knowing what to do becomes comically familiar and then suddenly terrifying, as if ordinary life could collapse at any moment into an existential nightmare. Now it becomes impossible to separate C from the narrator, also perched on a high rock, who is overtaken by C's anxiety, unless "it wasn't my own anxiety overtaking him?" (M, 6). For Beckett the ultimate question of how to live cries out in this intimate embrace between a writer and his fictional counterpart; call them both Molloy.

After "my soul's leap out to him, at the end of its elastic" (M, 7), the narrator turns his attention to the other, more urbane, man he calls A (or was it C? He forgets). His tone is cooler and more suspicious: "He moved with a kind of loitering indolence which rightly or wrongly seemed to me expressive" (M, 7). A dog follows, as Moran's son follows his father. Then the narrator's imagination takes hold of A's essential isolation. Perhaps the dog is a stray taken up into his arms from compassion or sheer loneliness. The later parts of Moran's narrative display just such fluctuations of lonely aloofness and need.

The narrator's pity for each of these proto-characters differs in color, but it does extend to both of them as they gradually disappear from sight. And so it is for Molloy and Moran. Moran first appears as a prototype of the bourgeois world Molloy fears and hides from: "They wake up hale and hearty, their tongues hanging out for order, beauty and justice, baying for their due" (M, 61). His mission, like that of the puppet characters in *Murphy*, is to track down Molloy, spy on him, and do something about him. If Molloy has doubts, Moran has habits, opinions, possessions, religion, and directives from a mythical employer. Nevertheless, Moran's search for Molloy is as confused and directionless as Molloy's own journey. Getting to Molloy's region is to uncover the Molloy-like being in himself. By the end of his narrative Moran has failed to complete his assigned mission, and is about as disabled as Molloy was at the beginning of his. He thinks he is done for, though he can't yet know what lies ahead. Back home, the hens and the bees and the servant he thought he possessed have crumbled away, making room for the beginnings of wonder and insecurity. In Beckett's sense, Moran is becoming a real person, on speaking terms with dying. He isn't there yet, but he has taken preliminary steps toward citizenship in Beckett's liminal world.

Part of the reader's entertainment in *Molloy* lies in picking up all the little details that Beckett strews like breadcrumbs to mark the overlapping mental and physical territories of his two characters. They range from elastic hat fasteners to violent attacks on men they encounter in the forest—men who mirror some rejected part of themselves. Molloy's victim is a lonely, needy figure who begs for his company; Moran's a smug, well-dressed detective in pursuit of another Molloy-like figure. In both cases rage momentarily triumphs over the characters' physical limitations as they kick or beat their opponents.

Beckett retains the individuality of the two even as he assimilates them. Moran still exists in a legal universe. He kills his man in a fit of unconscious violence, covers up the body, and hides his misdeed from his son. Molloy is at pains to explain in proud detail exactly how he kicked the other man by swinging his stiff legs to achieve the necessary momentum, while bracing himself on his crutches. He thinks nothing further of the encounter once he has sufficiently vented his rage in one last kick. Moran becomes less and less certain of who he is, but he never sounds like Molloy. To the end he feels himself uniquely heroic in his suffering, and congratulates himself for being a sly one, "wily as a serpent," after he cons an angry farmer with an implausible fiction (M, 168). Moran is probably supposed to represent an earlier phase of Molloy's decline, but his main effect on me is to cherish Molloy's asocial honesty all the more by contrast.

The endings of each narrative underline the distinctions. Moran's farewell to the reader is to snatch away everything he has told us. "Then I went back into the house and wrote, It is midnight. The rain is beating on the windows. It was not midnight. It was not raining" (M, 170). He's acting out a cruel and absolute version of Beckett's tendency to cast doubt on the truth of any narrative. Molloy's final sentences come as a relief after the incessant striving of his journey. In the ditch, unable to move without help, "I longed to go back into the forest. Oh not a real longing. Molloy could stay, where he happened to be" (M, 85). In that calm serenity, Molloy finds a momentary freedom from the imperative to find his mother, and from the requirement that he go on writing. The three short sentences take us from motion and emotion to a simple giving in, from first to third person. Beckett steps in at the last moment to set his character, and his fiction, gently down to rest.

In 1948, as Beckett was working on *Malone Dies*, he began an important new friendship with Georges Duthuit, an avant-garde writer and art critic who had revived the magazine *transition* after the war. Beckett made some money by doing translations for Duthuit, and they grew closer because of their mutual interest in the abstract paintings of their friend Bram van Velde. For a few years, Duthuit was the recipient of Beckett's most confidential letters, taking the place of Beckett's earlier confidant Thomas MacGreevy, whose devotion to things Irish had begun to separate the friends. Beckett's letters to Tom were now politely warm and informative in the rather upbeat style of catching up with an old acquaintance. It was Duthuit who was entrusted with the wilder parts of Beckett's thinking during those years of extraordinary artistic invention, and who received the troubled outpourings from Beckett's sojourns in Ireland. During his 1948 visit, Beckett imagined Duthuit as the soul-brother who would understand his identification with failure and his scorn for the literary circles of Dublin:

> But acceptance of ignorance, of pure weakness: for that one must look beyond the pen- or brush-holders. Here I hold my tongue. But the other evening, blinded by whiskey, I started to shout and make frantic gestures. My audience, the highly cultivated kind, brought me back in no time to decent behavior, with shoals of quotations from the usual untouchables. (*Letters*, 2:84–5)

Duthuit and his wife had met Beckett and Suzanne as a couple, and were among the few correspondents whom Beckett trusted with his anxieties about his companion, left alone in Paris. His mother, too, weighed on his conscience and his heart.

> I keep watching my mother's eyes, never so blue, so stupefied, so heartrending, eyes of an endless childhood, that of old age. Let us get there rather earlier, while there are still refusals we can make. I think these are the first eyes that I have seen. I have no wish to see any others, I have all I need for loving and weeping, I now know what is going to close, and open inside me, but without seeing anything, there is no more seeing. (*Letters*, 2:92)

I am moved by his ability to write "loving and weeping," a phrase perhaps released by his mother's loss of active power. Beckett, who inherited his mother's intensely blue eyes, blurs together all the eyes and tears, his mother's dying with his own. The nearly unintelligible images of opening and closing, seeing and not seeing, sketch out some inchoate emotional transition.

The travail in Ireland may have fed the darkness in Beckett's new work on *Malone Dies*, which charts the long dilution of a life now confined to a bed in a room. Malone wants to control the remainder of his course, as Beckett had hoped in his letter to encounter the end "while there are still refusals we can make." His new narrator is strung between two efforts of will: the will to die and the will to live. His problem, as he sees it at the outset, is to fill the time between the present of writing and the event of his death, as he lies in bed with his exercise book and his stub of a pencil. He wants to take charge of this twilight interlude by calculating the course of his writing so that it fits into the time allotted, over which, of course, he has no control. He is going to play, he says, by telling four stories in neutral tones to pass the time. The short sentences of his opening attempt follow that rule.

Like all Beckettian plans, this one falls apart. The four stories Malone sets for himself start to break down as soon as they are listed. As they evaporate, he talks more about his own situation, and the narrative expands into a contest between the wish to end and the yearning to hold onto every disappearing piece of his life. In Beckett's characteristic narrative shape, the initially opposing forces of dying and writing gradually come closer together, until they—almost—coincide.

Malone tells two stories about invented characters who are versions of his earlier selves, interspersing those tales with the story of his life in the room he's confined to. Beckett took the risk of writing a bad pseudo-realist novel in the sections about the youth of a character Malone calls Saposcat. Sapo's parents, and the Lamberts, a distressingly ugly farm family, are described from the outside in the kind of general narrative we might associate with nineteenth-century—perhaps Russian—writers. Malone had intended to use his stories to fend off the darkness of pain and depression, but he can barely force himself to write Sapo's story. "What tedium!" he exclaims, or "This is awful." Finally, in "mortal tedium," Malone gives up on the story, which has passed the time, but failed to keep darkness at bay (MD, 211).

Without the Sapo story, Malone's mind becomes chaotic, open to the kind of hallucinations that come and go during a certain stage of Parkinson's disease. He imagines sounds coming from the basement, the house full of people and babies. There's no one to tell him whether the sounds and the people are really there. "To conclude from this that I am a prey to hallucinations pure and simple is however a step I hesitate to take" (MD, 213). He describes at length, if incoherently, the shades of grey light in his room. Then the noises and people cease, leaving silence. Malone wonders if it has all been in his head, or if the head is actually his. His soul is agitated in its prison: "the soul that must be veiled, that soul denied in vain, vigilant, anxious, turning in its cage as in a lantern, in the night without haven of craft or matter or understanding. Ah yes, I have my little pastimes and they" (MD, 215). At this moment, when he hints that composing such sentences may be balm for that entrapped soul, he breaks off. Malone has lost his pencil stub.

Once he has managed to retrieve it, he writes about the forty-eight hours when the pencil was gone. His life has, after all, continued in the absence of writing. He lavishes description on the tiny stub his green pencil has become, as if its diminution is equivalent to his own. Malone won't use a new French pencil he claims to have in his bed, presumably because its newness is not a metaphor for his little remaining life. (The French pencil has to be a joke about the English translation we are reading.) Almost losing the exercise book is equally fraught with both terror and hope that the end has come.

Malone has completed the business of Sapo and feels, almost blissfully, on the verge of death. Yet he knows better. "And it is without excessive sorrow that I see us again as we are, namely to be removed grain by grain until the hand, wearied, begins to play, scooping us up and letting us trickle back into the same place, dreamily as the saying is" (MD, 218). The proverbial hourglass with its sand running out is transformed into an indifferent hand messing at random with the onward flow of deterioration in a human body. As his mother lay dying in 1950, Beckett found a related image in a letter about the fluctuations of her decline, "like the decrescendo of a train I used to listen to in the night at Ussy, interminable, starting up again just when one thinks it is over and silence restored for ever."[10] The daily alternations of hope and despair that come with watching a loved person die can generate that sense of helpless frustration.

Like the train, Malone starts up his storytelling again after this interlude, greeting with joy a new character he will call Macmann, a Molloy-like figure clad, like Beckett's father, in the signature green greatcoat. The coat and hat are described at loving length, and with obvious relief. Macmann is at a late stage of his wanderings, and he elicits a mode of empathic Beckettian storytelling that recalls Molloy, who never did get around to describing his hat and greatcoat as fully as he wished. The novel's second half alternates between Malone's story about Macmann and his own loss of control over his limbs. Macmann, according to Malone, is still in an earlier stage of life:

> [He] has still the whole of his old age before him, and then that kind of epilogue when it is not very clear what is happening and which does not seem to add very much to what has already been acquired or to shed any great light on its confusion, but which no doubt has its usefulness, as hay is left out to dry before being garnered.
>
> (MD, 225)

Here Beckett carries on his habit of extending the successive stages of old age that must be endured before death comes to garner the hay left to dry. A later stage generates a story about a previous stage, as Molloy's part seems to generate Moran's, or as the voice in *Rockaby* describes its dying woman before the moment she moves to her final position in the rocking chair. I find myself drawn to these sequences, because they want to reverse, or at least forestall, the death direction. Malone's narratives represent themselves as words filling up the time before the escape into death that never quite arrives. Yet there's a powerful countercurrent, a wish to move back into the greater scope of living that's been left behind. Is that the same as an autobiographical impulse? I will venture to say no: unlike the wish to turn past personal experience into narrative, it's more fundamental, like a gravitational pull toward life that's at least as powerful as the pull toward an end. When Malone muses "without excessive sorrow" about the hand that sometimes scoops up and replaces the sand before it can run out, he seems to be getting at the innate hope to survive that, willy-nilly, defies any desire to be finished with the business of living.

Malone thinks he is about to die many times over, and repeatedly panics about getting to the inventory of his possessions before his end comes.[11] Each time he resigns himself and turns back to Macmann's story, until a new disaster strikes: he loses the stick that allows him to draw his few possessions toward him, and he is left without attendance or food. At that critical juncture the engine of Macmann's tale starts up once again. He is now placed in a charitable asylum, where his experience begins to merge with Malone's. Sex enters the picture to enliven things for a while longer: Malone invents a long account of Macmann's affair with his equally aged carer Moll. It is Beckett sex: two ancient bodies working to create a bit of pleasure, the one attracted while the other is repulsed, and then the reverse. As he draws out Macmann's story, Malone becomes increasingly expressive about clinging to life. "Yes, there is no use pretending, it is hard to leave everything" (MD, 270).

In its endgame the story takes a violent turn. As if to smother the pain of losing human interest and care, the final episodes of Malone's story mount a ferocious attack on charity, with its regulations, statutes, and sullen or hypocritical agents. The villain who precipitates the final catastrophe is a dreadful society woman called Lady Petal, who prides herself on her benevolence. She insists on taking a group of badly disabled men from the asylum on an outing to an island, thinking—in Beckett's pitch-perfect parody—that she is "bringing a little happiness into the lives of others less fortunate than herself" (MD, 273). She carries on with criminal good cheer, oblivious to the fact that the trip is sheer torture for everyone. The denial and false optimism practiced by the caregiving professions in the face of real suffering and death never failed to upset Beckett. He ends Macmann's tale by taking revenge. In a flurry of action, the attendant Lemuel kills two of Lady Petal's sailors, leaves her alone and injured on the island, and throws his asylum charges into a boat that is last seen drifting in the bay, carrying huddled bodies that may, or may not, be dead. The rage and violence in this story find no relief.

Is the end of Macmann's story also the end of Malone's life? The only thing we're allowed to know is that it's the end of Malone's writing, which disintegrates into tiny phrases on the final page. Lemuel, it is said, will never again hit anyone with his bloody hatchet or—as his figure is superimposed on Malone's—"with his pencil or with his stick." Malone's story is gone, "never anything/ there/any more" (MD, 281). All of this is told in abrupt fragments by a storyteller who is hurrying up his ending.

More than a year after completing the manuscript, Beckett admitted to Mania Péron that he was not satisfied with the ending, even after he'd revised it. "It had to work actively, but not too much, not to the point of extinguishing the effort to end. Very difficult, And, not being there any more, I didn't manage it" (Letters, 2:303). Extinguishing the effort to end? Beckett may mean that the flurry of melodramatic action that disposes of his characters fails to give Malone an inner winding down that could signify some calming or acceptance. Instead, his pencil is identified with Lemuel's hatchet, an instrument of violence that cuts off life before it has reached its natural end. Beckett was right, I think, in his assessment. His conclusion is like the quick snuffing of a long-burning candle, before it can go out on its own.

During the composition of the trilogy, Beckett remained virtually unknown to any public beyond his circles of friends and fellow artists. Because of his diffidence about self-promotion, Suzanne acted as his agent, shopping his work around to publishers. It was not until 1950, after May Beckett died and Beckett completed *The Unnamable*, that Suzanne found Jérôme Lindon of Editions de Minuit, who would become Beckett's faithful French publisher. After *Molloy* was published in March 1951, Suzanne tactfully explained to Lindon that Beckett would not agree to the usual rituals of publicity. He would not be put up for prizes because of "the publicity which would then be directed, not only at his name and his work, but at the man himself" (*Letters*, 2:243). He would not give interviews.

> I fear that on this he is not to be budged. He gives his work, his role stops there. He cannot talk about it. That is his attitude. As for "his life," it is really not, as he sees it, worth a journalist's while to go out of his way to question him about it. (*Letters*, 2:245)

I hear Beckett's voice in Suzanne's words, as well as her understanding of the personal privacy he demanded in order to write. Beckett would later come to do his own explaining along these lines, but in this instance the scare quotes around "his life" are telling. What did it mean to "have" a life, anyway? Any account in words would be as untruthful as fiction; if his readers could not find him in his work, that was their problem.

Beckett, I like to imagine, may have been one of those people for whom life never seems entirely real. I am sometimes baffled to find myself in the midst of it, and cannot understand why I am here, what it's all supposed to mean, and how we all go on from day to day. The feeling that life is a strange dream that hovers about me has come upon me since childhood, when I occasionally found myself detached, watching my current doings in disbelief. For Beckett any similar experience of strangeness would be amplified by the sense that he was most fully alive when he was writing.

Molloy could be called a life story in the form of fictional autobiography, in which two invented narrators recount their immediate pasts. Both Molloy and Moran cast doubt on the truth of their assertions, but the form itself remains relatively intact. The other figures they encounter on their journeys are presented as if they were actually there. The writing in Malone's exercise book is like a journal, in which Malone records what's been happening in the room he lies in, and invents stories that help him pass the time as he wastes away. His fictions allow him to send parts of himself away into made-up characters who reveal and conceal Malone the author. The split between the fictional "I" and the fictional "he" is relatively straightforward, emphasized by paragraph breaks between the two modes of writing. These distinctions fall away in the final book of the trilogy. *The Unnamable* directly worries the dilemma of "life" and the words it generates to explain itself.

As *The Unnamable* opens, its narrator rejects all the people and things that show up in his earlier fictions. "All those Murphys, Molloys and Malones do not fool me. They have made me waste my time, suffer for nothing, speak of them when, in order to stop speaking, I should have spoken of me and me alone" (TU, 297). Although he is heavily burdened by an imperative to write, he hopes that removing all the fictional screens will allow him finally to achieve the silence he yearns for. He wants the suffering and pain he expressed through his surrogates to be given back to him, their only true source. I imagine the voice of the Unnamable as an attempt to conjure a being who lacks "a life," but lurks invisibly behind the words he produces. Always in hiding, he cannot be named. Yet his authorship is not singular. "To speak of me" requires that there is a subject who speaks and one, in the object position, who is spoken of.

To address that problem, the Unnamable creates another voice he calls Mahood. The name makes me think of a head covering or disguise, added to the first syllable of Malone.

> It was he told stories about me, lived in my stead, issued forth from me, came back to me, entered back into me, heaped stories on my head...his voice continued to testify for me, as though woven into mine, preventing me from saying who I was, what I was, so as to have done with saying, done with listening. (TU, 303)

Beckett is talking about the voice of a narrator, the voice on the page that cannot be identical with the author's being, though it emanates from and returns to it. In fact, the Unnamable asserts, the word producer would be fast asleep, and "from my sleeping mouth the lies would pour out, about me" (TU, 303). There is no way to speak only of me, who can only appear under the disguise of words originally fashioned by others.

Beckett began writing *The Unnamable* in a new space, a room in Ussy-sur-Marne that he and Suzanne had taken to get away from Paris. They would continue going to Ussy as a country retreat, eventually building a simple house where Beckett could write and be active outdoors. Not long after settling in there, Beckett wrote to Duthuit:

> I cycle frantically, I, that is the person who is supposed to represent me. The same poor fool nails, screws, saws and files, cursing and swearing, and happy. By far the best thing for him to do. And in front of the blank page he would like to be busy too, rush in to measure, foresee, prop up. But a bit shamefaced all the same, knowing it is not his place. (*Letters*, 2:150)

The split between I the writer and I the person living his domestic life looks clear at first, but proves as unstable in this paragraph as it was in the novel Beckett was writing. "I" is a word that represents Beckett, but "I" is quickly transformed into another. "He" doesn't belong at the writing table, though he would like to be planning the writing the way he is planning the arrangements of his house. The tiny vignette points to the mystery of the relation between a living writer and his narrative voices, which Beckett pursued at great length in *The Unnamable*.

As one might expect, it is not so easy to clear away all the trappings of fiction, to which the Unnamable is clearly attached. His attempts leave him stranded, because he knows nothing about himself except what he learns from his "delegates" (TU, 291), as the authorial part of a person learns about herself by looking at what she's written. It seems he will have to resort to fairy tale again. Mahood is the alleged narrator of fictions, but on the sentence level the Unnamable and Mahood blur in and out of one another, as if they are competing on the page for control of the telling voice. The first fairy tale Mahood tells is based on the myth of Ulysses returning to wife and family after a long absence. We hear the voices of waiting family members speaking of "he," as they observe the slow approach of a decrepit one-legged figure. "That's one of Mahood's favorite tricks, to produce independent testimony in support of my historical existence," the Unnamable jokes (TU, 312). On the other hand, he soon wonders "if I was not in fact the creature revolving in that yard, as Mahood assured me" (TU, 314). It's clearly impossible to untangle the loops that entwine author with narrative voice.

Mahood's second tale is a comic fantasy, which places "I" in a large jar situated in the shambles of a town not unlike Molloy's. He is cared for by the owner of a chop-house across the street, a woman who takes on the caretaking role. She empties his jar once a week, gives him bones to suck on, and covers him with a tarpaulin when it snows. In return, he serves as a landmark for her restaurant, "far more effective than for example a chef in cardboard, pot-bellied in profile and full face wafer thin" (TU, 322). She props up the jar on a pedestal and places a menu under his nose. This comical absurdity acquires realistic details in the jar-dweller's down-to-earth speculations about the woman's intentions, her menus, and the urban passers-by, until the Unnamable exclaims, "This story is no good, I'm almost beginning to believe it" (TU, 323). He has created a fantastical situation and made it "real" by treating it as if it were a normal life arrangement that generates its own rather lovable human observations, anxieties, and hopes. The special blend of comedy and pathos is closer to the mood of *Molloy* than to *Malone Dies*.

The interplay with Mahood is only the simplest of the unresolvable contradictions Beckett will introduce as *The Unnamable* goes on. For this work he had set himself the impossible task of writing a non-representational novel in which most assertions are ignored, negated, or revised, and all distinctions blur into one another.

That may sound like the bleakest of the bleak, but—as in the instance of the man in the jar—I laughed out loud quite often as I read *The Unnamable*. Because I grew to understand it as an exploration of a writer's relationship with words, the work invited me into a puzzle so various and intricate that it was impossible not to be drawn in by it.

In letters to Duthuit dated March 1949, during the interval between finishing *Waiting for Godot* and beginning *The Unnamable*, Beckett struggled to express something about new directions for art, using the abstract paintings of Bram van Velde as his springboard. He was collaborating with Duthuit on a dialogue about contemporary painters, published that year in *transition* under the title *Three Dialogues*. Based on his identification with Bram's ambitions and his equally personal despair of them, Beckett was attempting to theorize about the impossibility of expression. Much of his intellectual thrashing is difficult to follow, but a long letter of March 9, 1949 raises a few of the enormous questions Beckett was asking. Like other letters to Duthuit, this one takes his skepticism to extremes. "And if not, can one conceive of expression in the absence of relations of whatever kind, whether those between 'I' and 'non-I' or those within the former?" (*Letters*, 2:139).

Beckett tries momentarily to imagine an art that does not depend on "relations," whether they are relations between the inner world and the outer, between the self and another, or between the self and the self. At the same time he knows that he can see "Bram's case" only as a version of his own, that Bram is a figure, like the characters in his novels, that allows him to speak, in indirect autobiography, about something in himself. "And I shall tend irresistibly to pull Bram's case over towards my own, since that is the condition of being in it and talking about it, and then for other reasons less easy to admit" (*Letters*, 2:139). Bram cannot be discussed without a relation to himself. The "I give up" gesture that ends the letter is also a direct appeal to Duthuit's importance as an interlocutor: "I am no longer capable of writing *about*. So, if you are not altogether sick of me, you are going to have to ask me questions. I shall try to answer. But bear in mind that I who hardly ever talk about myself talk about little else" (*Letters*, 2:141). That last sentence is, I think, an explanation of what Beckett meant when he wrote of "reasons less easy to admit." The art of painting, which had taken hold of his imagination during his youthful fascination with the Irish painter Jack Butler Yeats, had always been a screen on which he could project his own obscure sense of the artist's relationship with the non-human world. He knew it, though he was reluctant to admit outright to the implicit egoism. In those perfectly characteristic last sentences to Duthuit, Beckett's honesty prevails: he knows that writers write themselves no matter how assiduously they conceal the autobiographical impulse.

Art without relations is, after all, impossible. The letter itself exists only because of his relations with Bram van Velde and with Georges Duthuit, its recipient. Beckett's friendship, both self-deprecatory and trusting, is always aware of how his interlocutor might respond to him. In the same way he would arrange his fictive situations so that speaking occurs only if there is a listener, reader, or recorder of some sort. Even if you understood art as a failed attempt to express yourself, the failure had to be addressed *to* another being.

The Unnamable's biggest antagonist is an entity that's referred to only as "they." "They" are the ones that bring up children and teach them language. Like the anonymous "they" who insist that

Molloy write his story, they demand writing, and they try to control it. Although they take different forms at different moments in the novel, they seem to be vague personifications of the critical world and its belief in words. They threaten the Unnamable's desire to achieve perfect silence and rest by reaching a "me." He is condemned by language to produce more language, which sometimes sickens him, as if words from somewhere else poured into one ear and came out of his mouth without his agency. "They" also want to entrap him into writing about himself, a self with an ego: "Do they believe I believe it is I who am speaking? That's theirs too. To make me believe I have an ego all my own and can speak of it, as they speak of theirs. Another trap to snap me up among the living" (TU, 339). "They"—like the journalists who wanted to interview Beckett—are engaged in all manner of feints to make the narrator confess to being a man.

In the midst of the long struggle against the forces of "they," a new entity emerges to replace Mahood as a surrogate. This is Worm, who relieves the Unnamable of the necessity for saying "I" by giving him one more story to tell. Worm is the ultimate "creature": a non-human, non-mammal, non-speaking, faceless bit of living matter—almost as far from human culture as you can get. But not for long. In a wonderfully comic series of projections, the Unnamable sets about creating Worm in his own image. His obvious delight in doing this is infectious. When he says "the rascal, he's getting humanized, he's going to lose if he doesn't watch out," the affectionate voice is irresistible (TU, 353).

As Worm becomes a full-blown autobiographical surrogate, the Unnamable recounts Worm's life in the womb, already helplessly assailed by human talk about how he's progressing. He imagines Worm attempting to resist "their" ideas of him.

The reader watches as the Unnamable, in a torrent of "perhaps" and "if" possibilities, keeps revising his notion of what Worm is and can do. Is it the writer or "they" who are dragging Worm into the human race? Unclear, but the Unnamable begins to wish for Worm's company: "How pleasant it would be if he had a face," and could appear as a visitor (TU, 356). He's sucked into wanting more for Worm's future: perhaps he could grasp time, learn how to count. It's delightful, good-humored play with the process of invention, as it goes about creating a fellow being from almost nothing. The affectionate tone is charmingly prolonged in a 1951 letter from Ussy to Mania Péron:

> Between the April showers I scratch the mud and observe the worms, an observation entirely devoid of scientific detachment. I try not to hurt them, with the spade. All the while knowing that, cut into two, they at once fashion a new head, or a new tail, whichever is the case. (Letters, 2:241)

Once Worm has faded from the narrative, the Unnamable goes a bit mad, producing long segments of repetitious circularity, written in sentences that go on and on before reaching an endpoint. Sometimes they feel like a driver frantically revving his engine, spinning his wheels when his car is badly stuck in the mud. It's the closest he can get to uttering language that doesn't represent anything. At times he sounds like Lucky's crazy forced speech in Waiting for Godot; the voice becomes hysterical, then pretends to reason. With a canny sense of how much a reader can tolerate, Beckett brings us out of these tailspins for brief comic interludes. Mahood and Worm return for short runs. "They" try to convince the Unnamable that he has an identity by producing a photograph, along with police and medical records. He gives himself orders about how to proceed sensibly with his writing, but the orders are quickly revoked in a bout of nostalgic feeling. Then he rehearses the plot of a melodrama that ends in unnecessary deaths; this, he claims, was supposed to teach him about emotion and endings. Each burst of material, soon dispensed with, stumbles toward another. The effort becomes exhausting, and leaves the reader wishing, like the narrator, for silence to begin.

The closing phrases of *The Unnamable*—"you must go on, I can't go on, I'll go on"—may be the most frequently quoted lines in Beckett (TU, 407). Just two months into writing the novel, Beckett confessed to Duthuit that he'd done something he'd never done before:

> I wrote the last page of the book I am working on, whereas I am only on my 30th. I am not proud of myself. But the outcome is already so little in doubt, whatever the writings that lie between me and it, of which I have only the vaguest of ideas. (*Letters*, 2:162)

His embarrassment recalls his early attack on Balzac's calculated control of his narratives, in *Dream of Fair to Middling Women*. In published form, the famous end phrases are the last words of a sentence that goes on for five and a half closely printed pages before reaching the period that ends the novel. The voice has acquired a kind of calm, as it slowly revolves around the idea of reaching a silence in which "I" might be free of imprisonment by words. Yet perhaps that silence "is not worth having, that's all I know, it's not I, that's all I know," because words have not yet found the "me" he wanted to speak of (TU, 407). For all its uncertainty, the ending is not a whipping to arms in the face of defeat. To my ears, it sounds like a moving acceptance of what has been written, with hopes for what remains to write. If *The Unnamable* were a piece of music, the ending might be marked *tranquillo*, after the *agitato* of earlier portions.

you must say words, as long as there are any, until they find me, until they say me, strange pain, strange sin, you must go on, perhaps it's done already, perhaps they have said me already, perhaps they have carried me to the threshold of my story, before the door that opens on my story, that would surprise me, if it opens, it will be I, it will be the silence, where I am, I don't know, I'll never know, in the silence you don't know, you must go on, I can't go on, I'll go on.

4

IN THE MUD

It is so much simpler to be hurt than to hurt.
                    —Samuel Beckett to Thomas McGreevy, December 22, 1937

When 31-year-old Beckett wrote that sentence, he was confiding a private humiliation he'd endured from James Joyce. Joyce had paid him too little for fifteen hours of proofreading work, and "then supplemented it with an old overcoat and 5 ties! I did not refuse" (*Letters*, 1:574). A small thing, but emblematic of the way Joyce treated those who dedicated good parts of their lives to helping him, as Beckett had done for some years. Hand-me-downs from Joyce were just what Beckett did not need, as he strove toward developing a literary voice of his own. But he swallowed the hurt as he did others, trained perhaps at his mother's knee. The alternative was to make a fuss, create conflict, and widen the pain beyond his stoical self. That was not Beckett's way; he was too prone to feel guilty about hurting any living being. His aggressions were generally limited to fierce defenses of his work and privacy, or to sudden acts of violence that appeared out of the blue in his fiction, leaving no residue of guilt. But, after the years of war and the literary successes of the 1950s, the simplicity of his 1937 formula gave way to a very different vision of the violence that lurks in love.

Beckett finished *The Unnamable* in 1950. Nine years later, it was still haunting him. By then he was famous, both for the three novels and for what amounted to a new, public, European-American career as a playwright for theater and radio. His letters are full of arrangements for publication or performance, explanations to directors, rehearsal woes, and permissions for excerpts to be published in magazines or read on BBC radio. In the face of all this outreach and sociability, his need to restore himself by retreating to solitary work in his Ussy-sur-Marne cottage became ever stronger. From "my hole in the Marne mud," he would tell friends that he spent much of his outdoor time digging holes for new trees he intended to plant (*Letters*, 2:584). The physical labor was an outlet, a way to let off steam when he was tired and frustrated in writing or translation. The mud itself was a metaphor. "Work nil." Beckett reported to Georges Duthuit in January 1952. "The anchor is firmly in, and with each lurch sinks a little deeper into the mud. If it goes on like this I shall have to find another pastime" (*Letters*, 2:311). He feared that *The Unnamable* had been the end of the line for his writing. The mood lingered; late in 1958 Beckett was telling Barney Rosset, his American publisher at Grove Press,

> I feel I'm getting more and more involved in professionalism and self-exploitation and that it would be really better to stop altogether than to go on with that. What I need is to get back into the state of mind of 1945 when it was write or perish. But I suppose no chance of that.[1]

Self-exploitation? Beckett dismisses his work in theater and translation as if he were deliberately fabricating a public face that betrayed the more important part of himself. Did he imagine writing for theater as a kind of prostitution? His deep suspicion of success in human endeavor revived fond memories of his impoverished and anonymous past, when he'd just begun to break new ground in *Molloy*.

The Unnamable remained crucial to Beckett, years after its publication. I would guess that he saw it as a true breakthrough, perhaps as his most definitive transformation of the novel form into something new. It had been an attempt to do without place, character, time passing, or even a clear direction toward death. It used words to disqualify language itself. And yet it was moving and varied in its emotional tones, propelling itself forward, like music, through shifts of mood and tempo. None of this was possible on the stage, which would always retain, at minimum, a visible body or two.

In April 1951, after Jérôme Lindon had agreed to publish all three novels, Beckett thanked him for his eagerness to get to the manuscript of *L'Innommable*.

> As I told you, it is this last work that I am most attached to, although it has left me in a sorry state. I'm trying to get over it. But I am not getting over it. I do not know if it will be able to make a book. Perhaps it will all have been for nothing.   (*Letters*, 2:234)

He had already begun to write some very short prose pieces that he described to one correspondent as "A bit torn off the placenta *of L'Innommable*," to another as a "twitching," as if the pieces were the last convulsions of a corpse (*Letters*, 2:263, 285). Beckett couldn't stop writing *The Unnamable*. Perhaps he was ensuring that he could save something of the novel in the event that it "will all have been for nothing"— much as pieces of *Dream of Fair to Middling Women* had been preserved in *More Pricks Than Kicks*.

The short texts are packed and powerful in themselves, individual in tone, and mind-breaking like the progenitor novel. They worry the same dilemmas: that language cannot touch an under-lying "me;" that "he" and "I" are tangled together in a knot that can't be untied. In early 1954 Beckett described the pieces to Barney Rosset as "thirteen or fourteen very short abortive texts (Textes pour Rien) that express the failure to implement the last words of *L'Innommable*: il faut continuer, je vais continuer" (*Letters*, 2:457). He was still beating himself up over this, as he had been doing since finishing the last little text. Thirteen of them would be collected under the title *Textes pour Rien*, and published in 1955 along with the three short stories written in 1946.

Inevitably, the time came for Beckett to translate *L'Innommable* into English. That meant climbing back into every detail of the work that was still chastising his conscience. On March 12, 1956 Beckett wrote to his American friend Pamela Mitchell: "My God how I hate my own work. Have started the impossible job of trans-lating L'Innommable and gave it up the other day in loathing. Shall be fifty (50) in a month's time and can well believe it. 18,000 days and not much to show for it" (*Letters*, 2:606). This kind of depres-sive thinking becomes familiar to any reader of Beckett's letters, especially when he's writing to women he cares for. During the 1950s that mood is prominent, despite the new achievements of that decade: the many productions of *Waiting for Godot* in several countries and languages, the difficult new play *Endgame*, the popu-lar *Krapp's Last Tape*, and the first two radio plays, *All That Fall* and *Embers*. *Krapp's Last Tape* was written in a kind of exuberance, to celebrate completing a draft translation of *The Unnamable* in early 1958. Krapp's memory monologue, which Beckett described iron-ically to Donald McWhinnie as "rather a sentimental affair in my best original English manner," seems to have delighted him (*Letters*, 3:115). He told Jacoba (Tonny) van Velde that the play "is pleasantly sad and sentimental: a nice little entrée of artichoke hearts, to be followed by the tripe à la shit of Hamm and Clov. People will say, Well, well, he has blood in his veins, who would have thought it, must be age" (*Letters*, 3:131). The comic muse had not deserted him; Krapp and his plaintive Irish memories had cheered him up. Always conscious of how audiences would respond to his work, he saw that Krapp's emotional colloquy with his past selves would serve as a useful curtain opener to ease the harshness of his one-act play *Endgame*.

Translating *The Unnamable* did not quiet its ghost. Beckett could not get over the idea that he should be writing another long French prose work that would move his art forward. On February 3, 1959 he confided to his old friend Con Leventhal: "I have given up all thought of theatre and radio and am struggling to struggle on from where the Unnamable left me off, that is with the next next to nothing" (*Letters*, 3:194). Writing plays and figuring out ingenious details of staging was compelling, but the more inward mission of prose writing also demanded its due. The work he'd begun to puzzle out would become *Comment C'Est*, or *How It is*.

His American producer, Alan Schneider, was at work on staging *Krapp's Last Tape* when Beckett told him not to be in a hurry. "There will be no theatre or radio from me now until I have done something that goes on from The Unnamable and Texts for Nothing or decided there is no going on from there for me, either of which operations will take a long time probably" (*Letters*, 3:209). By January 1960 Schneider heard a sadder account of the play: "Krapp has nothing to talk to but his dying self and nothing to talk to him but his dead one" (*Letters*, 3:277). A starker variation of the same need for an interlocutor was central to the new prose work.

In early May 1959 he had outlined its situation for Barney Rosset: "It all 'takes place' in the pitch dark and the mud, first part 'man' alone, second with another, third alone again. All a problem of rhythm and syntax and weakening of form, nothing more difficult." He was lashing himself to the mast of difficulty, intent on resisting the "siren voices" of theater and radio (*Letters*, 3:230).

I was shocked and depressed when I read *How It Is* for the first time. I told myself that I couldn't stomach a story about a naked creature in the mud who comes upon another like himself, and tortures the other's body with a tin-opener to make him speak, or to shut him up. Eventually the scene of forced speech broadens into a chain of endless like encounters, as each victim propels himself off through the mud until he finds another whom he can torture as he's been tortured. This relentless vision said to me that inflicting and bearing pain lies at the heart of all intimate relationships. Violence pops up suddenly in many of Beckett's works—think of what Molloy and Moran do to men encountered in the forest, or the murders at the end of *Malone Dies*—but it has no legal or psychological consequences. It erupts, and disappears, like a sudden burst of rage. *How It Is*, on the other hand, includes prolonged and precise descriptions of pain deliberately inflicted on a passive human body.

As usual, Beckett was onto my reaction. After the novel was finished, Patrick Magee, Beckett's best male interpreter, was slated to perform an excerpt for BBC radio. Beckett wrote an anticipatory apology: "I have never committed anything—I trust—so exhausted and unpalatable and shall not be in the least offended if you refuse to have anything to do with it" (*Letters*, 3:306). When Donald McWhinnie worried about Magee's reaction to the proposed reading, Beckett sympathized: "To read that in private is asking too much of anyone, let alone in public. I simply had nothing else to offer them" (*Letters*, 3:326).

My reluctance to touch *How It Is* was the extreme case of a pattern that developed in my reading of Beckett's work. I would call it a process of overcoming: my first encounter with a particular piece might put me off, either because of its painful content or because I couldn't find a way to make sense of the narrative. I would leave it for a while, feeling the emotional residue it left behind. When I returned, I wanted to figure it out: how was it made? What was its shape? What new experiments had Beckett come up with? In the course of re-reading, I would come to delight in those brilliant sentences that take language into unexpected, or funny, or tender turns. Read for the pleasure of its fluctuating moods and tones of voice, *How It Is* was not quite so unpalatable as Beckett had feared, and I had to admit that the work opened new territory. I decided to brave the mud and write about it, especially when I saw personal and political contexts that helped me to humanize this radical text.

First among them is Beckett's involvement in the controversy about torture that accompanied the years of the Algerian War of Independence (1954–62). The right-wing arm of the French military used torture and terrorism against thousands who fought as part of the Algerian National Liberation Front. In retaliation, the Algerian rebels tortured fellow Algerians who were pro-French or uncommitted to their cause. In *How It Is*, this cruel tit for tat is ironically referred to as justice.

The outrage in France came close to home for Beckett and Suzanne, who followed radio reports of the war with dismay. "Dreadful week, the two of us with ears glued to Europe No. 1

every hour. Things a little quieter now," Beckett reported in early 1960 (*Letters*, 3:294). Jérôme Lindon courageously published several books that testified to instances of torture, or appealed to French soldiers to desert in protest. He went on trial for inciting military disobedience, causing his friends a great deal of anxiety. Beckett actively supported a petition in support of Lindon that was signed by writers, publishers, and theater people. In the end it was too risky for him to sign as a foreigner, but he was close to French friends who suffered work losses because they were signatories.[2] In the oblique form of fiction, Beckett could put something of a signature on his own horror.

The 1950s also brought a personal crucible. In 1954 Beckett had a brief romantic affair with Pamela Mitchell, a lively American woman he had met when she was sent by her agency to obtain English-language rights to *Godot*. He and Suzanne Deschevaux-Dumesnil were still living in the tiny apartment they had shared since their relationship began. Beckett tried to warn Pamela that being with him was nothing but trouble for her, but the affair did not break off until Beckett left for Ireland as his brother Frank lay dying there. He and Mitchell continued to correspond long afterwards.

As it turned out, that affair was a prelude to a more lasting relationship with Barbara Bray, an English woman who worked with producer Donald McWhinnie as script editor for the BBC radio plays. She and Beckett met in 1958 and became a productive creative team, as well as personal intimates. A critic and translator in her own right, Bray would move to Paris in 1961 after she left her position at the BBC. In that same year, Beckett and Suzanne married secretly in England, and settled into a larger Paris apartment that allowed them each more private space. The two relationships went on in parallel for the rest of their lives. Beckett suffered from the pain he was causing both women; the man who hated the idea of cutting an earthworm with a spade did not want to think of his own cruelty to people he cared for and needed in different ways. "There's nothing to be done for me," he told Barbara, "except to try and see me as I am. You speak of the happiness one gives and gets. The situation I see is one where no matter what I do, pain will ensue somewhere for someone" (*Letters*, 3:285).

He persisted in trying to give each woman her due, refusing Barbara's requests to make some definite plan about what would and would not happen. His life was now multiply divided in two: his relationship in French and his relationship in English, his drama and his fiction, his writing and his self-translation, his busy life in Paris and his increasingly solo time at Ussy-sur-Marne.

Beckett's letters to Barbara Bray are special reading pleasures. His trust in her devotion and her literary judgment creates an ease in which he can move almost at random from one thing to another with the assurance that she would follow him. He sent her his work-in-progress, and told her how it was developing, with a confidence he displayed to no other correspondent. He read and commented on the many books she sent to him. Whatever the frequency of their actual meetings may have been, the meeting of minds persisted. It's through a letter to Bray that I learned about the new look of the pages in *How It Is*. In January 1960, well along in the process of writing and rewriting its three parts, Beckett noted,

> I think the set-up of part III is an improvement—opens the whole thing up and makes future insertions and adjustments much easier. Have next to see whether I can do the same thing with I–II. The extracts you have read—break it all up into brief packets, anything

from seven lines to one, with space between them, not easy because
of all the conjunctival elements to be got rid of.   (*Letters*, 3:285)

Arrived at rather late in the game, this decision makes all the
difference. For his next step forward, Beckett had decided to elim-
inate sentences. Getting rid of "all the conjunctival elements"—
everything that connects one word to another in the structure of
the sentence—was surely not easy, though it appealed to Beckett's
instinct to pare down as much as possible. The small packets of
prose, like poetic stanzas, make it possible to concentrate on each
separate burst of writing. The focus can change from one small
stanza to the next, so the white spaces on the page make it easier
to adjust to the shifts. Because there is no punctuation or capital-
ization, the reader has to become an active participant in creating
the rhythms of the narrative voice. To discern where each phrase
within a packet begins and ends, we have to hear the intonations
of speech in our own heads. In that way we are allied with the fiction Beckett establishes: that the man murmuring his words into
the mud is quoting a voice that comes from some inaccessible
place inside him, "an ancient voice in me not mine."[3]

Scattered throughout, the phrases "I quote" or "I say it as I hear
it" insist that the ancient voice is not identical with the recorded
words, which convey only a fraction of what might have been
said. Unlike the Unnamable, this narrator says he no longer cares
about the problem of who is speaking: "I hear and don't deny
don't believe don't say any more who is speaking that's not said
any more it must have ceased to be of interest" (HII, 21). He is now
interested in the "rags" or "fragments" of feeling and image that
come to him, captured in the form of those brief narrative packets.

The three parts of the narrative—before Pim, with Pim, and
after Pim—announce themselves as a kind of autobiography.

They "divide into three a single eternity for the sake of clarity" (HII, 24), as if a temporal plot line could divide an eternity. This so-called "natural order" collapses as soon as it's announced, because present, past, and future can't be disentangled in the telling. The human mind does not work in chronological order; it superimposes one time of life on another, in anticipation, dread, reminiscence, or hope. The overall organization draws us into a forward momentum, which leads from isolation toward a special relationship with the fellow creature he names Pim, and then to a long meditation on those events. The tripartite plan is regularly repeated as a refrain that tries helplessly to rope forays into past and future back into the chronological framework of the whole.

The physical aspect of solitary life in the mud is a central concern of Part I. Because there is no light, touch and sound are the operative senses. The mud extends throughout the visible world, as if earth and sky had been reduced to a single moist element compounded of soil and water. You can't dig holes in it; you can't walk on it, but it will hold you up if you lie on it face down, or curl up on your side. Locomotion forward is possible, with difficulty: "Push pull the leg straightens the arm bends all those joints are working the head arrives alongside the hand flat on the face and rest" (HII, 19). And again, starting on the other side. In this way ten or fifteen yards can be traversed. We are once again inside Beckett's method of comedic pathos, where a fantastical situation is made real through the adaptive human details it gives rise to.

The narrator's sole possession is a sack closed with a cord, which contains tins of sardines or prawns and a tin-opener. We learn, in detail, that it is extremely awkward to prop yourself on your elbows in the mud in order to reach into the sack to count the remaining tins; even more awkward to bring one out and open it.

Needless to say, food is a lifeline, and the anxious question hovers as to whether it will suffice. For an eternity? Will he lose the tin-opener in the mud? The narrator calms himself with the thought that his appetite will diminish more quickly than his tins will disappear. The greater consolation is that the sack is a love object, a pillow for his head or a thing to cuddle in his arms while lying curled up on his side. "I take it in my arms talk to it put my head in it rub my cheek on it lay my lips on it turn my back on it turn to it again clasp it to me again say to it thou thou" (HII, 17). In Beckett's art even a sack of edgy sardine tins can be transformed into a love story, complete with turning toward and turning away. When Pim arrives on the scene, the sack will disappear, as the fluctuations of rejection and desire intensify in an I-thou exchange.

Ambivalent pairings multiply in images of the narrator's past, which come to him in flashes from an earlier life above, in the light. These "rags of life in the light" include, remarkably, one that refers to a Suzanne-like figure sewing near his work table. She "sits aloof ten yards fifteen years looks at me says at last to herself all is well he is working." But his head is resting on the table, not asleep; she can see light and shadow pass with the winds. Though he doesn't move, he hopes she will call his name and come to him; but she grows anxious, "suddenly leaves the house and runs to friends" (HII, 10–11). This little passage is the most explicit reference to the everyday tugs of a domestic emotional life that I have come across in Beckett's work. She is content when he is safely writing; anxious if he is not. He wants her attention, but she runs away into a life of her own.

The other rags of memory also hint at close relationships. They include a scene in which a young child is praying at his mother's knee, based on a photograph of Beckett with his mother May; a brief glimpse of a boy with a man in tears; and an awkward adolescent love scene, in which the narrator and the girl stand back to back holding hands, while a dog cavorts absurdly on the leash held by the girl's other hand. Flashes of earthly beauty, clouds and sky float by, as well as a passage recalled from Beckett's story "The End," in which the narrator tries to nurture a crocus in a pot on his basement windowsill by moving it with a string so it will stay in the sunlight.[4] In its new context, that detail becomes a metaphor for all the instances of light from above that flash into the narrator's mind amid the underground darkness of How It Is.

Though the few remaining glimpses of past life are murmured indistinctly into the mud, the narrator announces on the first page that they must be saved by someone else who listens and records: "recorded none the less its preferable somehow somewhere as it stands as it comes my life my moments not the millionth part all lost nearly all someone listening another noting or the same" (HII, 7). Later Beckett embodies the recorder in two characters: a witness with a good lamp to observe, and a scribe to write down the proceedings. His need to be seen and recognized clings to his memories of human connections in a former life, and to those of his solitary life in the mud. The "dearness" of lost lives becomes more explicit as the section begins to wind down, with hints of nostalgia for the earlier time.

Anticipations of Part II haunt Part I with angst. The narrator sometimes sounds desperate for a companion's sounds and words, and sees himself crawling towards Pim. But the foreshadowing signs are not encouraging. We hear about "the words of Pim his extorted voice," with its hints of torture to come (HII, 21). The narrator mourns "the morale at the outset before things got out of hand satisfactory ah the soul I had in those days the equanimity that's why they gave me a companion" (HII, 25). Before the narrator's hand physically touches Pim's naked buttocks in the final lines of Part I, there are suggestions that he is about to lose his equanimity, perhaps even his soul.

Part II starts out on a high note. The utter darkness does not allow the narrator to see Pim, so he moves delicately to learn about the new creature by brushing his fingers over the parts of his body. He concludes that Pim is a little old man like himself, someone to touch and embrace as they lie side by side. It is a "happy time in its own way," as his hand lands "even with a touch of ownership already on the miraculous flesh" (HII, 51); "it's like my sack when I had it still this providential flesh I'll never let it go" (HII, 55). Although this early burst of romance is said to last "a vast stretch of time" in a timeless realm, it's not long before the sheer comfort of physical closeness and the dream of a lifelong partnership turn to something else. Pim suddenly sings a little tune. The discovery that he has a voice and language—perhaps he's singing a Lied in German or Italian!—changes everything. With "a human voice there within an inch or two," the narrator who murmurs into the mud now transfers to Pim the voice he needs to tell his own story (HII, 56). In order to fulfill this function, Pim has to be trained.

The methods are cruel and hard to read. The narrator starts by manipulating Pim's body at will, and tries to drill his name into him, much like a colonizer with an indigenous subject. The lessons to follow start with digging his long sharp nails into Pim's armpit to make him cry. When he does, his face gets shoved into the mud to shut him up. Pim learns that if he sings instead of crying, he will not be shut up, until he is silenced by a thump on the skull. Then the tin-opener comes into play, jabbed into Pim's buttock cheeks, and finally into his kidney. That generates speech. To force Pim to narrate his story—the one the narrator wants him to tell—he begins to carve Roman capital letters in blood on Pim's back, telling him what he must talk about. This Kafka-like horror show is an effort to turn a living being into a ventriloquist's dummy whose faked voice is run by the commands of his master. The awful details of Pim's training are interspersed with sympathetic descriptions of what Pim must be thinking, memories or anticipations of good moments, and overtones of love. The narrator is anxious to preserve Pim for his own use, so he avoids the worst things he can think to do to him. He often sidesteps, delaying the subject of torture by veering off into other fantasies.

What is this all about? Pim is another of Beckett's surrogate speakers, the next incarnation after Mahood in *The Unnamable*, who is brought into action to tell the author's stories for him. This time, however, Beckett emphasizes the painful extraction of narrative rather than the stories themselves. My initial response to *How It Is* points to the difference: this relationship between voices is now rendered as an intimate, partly sadistic, bodily encounter. The life in common shared by the narrator and Pim is a physical life.

Why did Beckett do this? I ask myself. The answers I come up with suggest several layers of preoccupation: political, interpersonal, and Beckett's own writing dilemma. The master–slave dynamic in encounters between colonizers and colonized peoples was on his mind because of the Algerian War. The interpersonal pain that emerges from sexual and domestic relationships was all too evident as he composed *How It Is* amid the stress of sustaining his involvement with two women. "They never quite kill the thing they think they love, lest their instinct for artificial respiration should go abegging," Beckett had written in *Murphy*, but this time the amalgam of love and violence is not confined to women (*Murphy*, 202–3).

Some of Beckett's grief lay in his battle to express these matters at all. Throughout his work he'd been engaged in a push-me-pull-you dynamic whenever he began to talk about love or need. When he let such feelings emerge, he'd quickly find a way to counter them, either through narrators who claim not to know what love is, or by changing the subject. Like a glimpse of emotional depth that is quickly covered up, such moments paradoxically dramatize inner privacy and assert the sanctity of feelings that should not be misrepresented by commonly uttered words. An extreme case, *How It Is* presents a disturbing brew of stark human need laced with hostility.

Part III takes us out of the encounter with Pim, into the mind of a narrator who behaves like someone traumatized by a previous experience. He can't move on from it, so he expands and multiplies the tormenter–victim duo into an endless chain of succession, imagining untold numbers of bodies moving through the mud toward their next victims, loving and torturing until the victims abandon them and swim away to inflict the same pain on the next victim. The single relationship is generalized to a universal curse, a chase after intimacy that inevitably brings betrayal and abandonment. Narrative time expands to the period before Part I and after Part III, as the narrator imagines himself in an earlier relation to another called Bom and sees a repetition of that encounter in what would be the unwritten Part IV.

There are moments of emotion when the need to "cleave" to another and the sorrow of abandonment come through, but much of the section is distanced through intellectual games with numbers. Now it's 5,000, then 100,000, then a "a thousand thousand nameless solitaries half abandoned, half abandoning" (HII, 115–16). Yet each re-encounter with the same partner feels like the first time: "and these same couples that eternally form and form again all along this immense circuit that the millionth time that's conceivable is as the inconceivable first and always two strangers uniting in the interests of torment" (HII, 121). The numbers keep rising and falling, as if we were in a Wonderland where things shrink and expand without explanation. The narrator seems to console himself for his guilty participation in the endless round by making his activities a small instance of a universal series that can't be escaped.

Before he can end, the narrator has to put himself through several other mathematical games: if all the leavings and joinings occur simultaneously, how can the times and distances be determined? How is it that the sacks are taken away, and by whom, at the correct moment in each body's journey? Who has been organizing the whole scenario? As we might expect from Beckett, one of his closing efforts is to dismiss everything that's been written as a fantasy emanating from just a single voice.

As this section put itself through its paces, I imagined the narrative as a kind of cow that chews and regurgitates the same fodder, until the repetitions begin to wane or merge in almost unreadable ways. The narrator's withdrawal to a universalizing distance can release bursts of pity and sorrow: "so on and similarly all along the chain in both directions for all our joys and sorrows we extort and endure from one another from one to the other" (HII, 141). Yet the mechanical aspect of the romantic chase appears to be obligatory, "involving for one and all the same obligation precisely that of fleeing without fear while pursuing without hope" (HII, 43).

It was, apparently, only through extremities of mud and torment that Beckett could express the guilty urgency of the human need for other bodies and voices. However unwillingly extorted, they are said to be more nourishing than the tins of food that provide imaginary consolation at the beginning of the novel: "for the likes of us and no matter how we are recounted there is more nourishment in a cry nay a sigh torn from one whose only good is silence or in speech extorted from one at last delivered from its use than sardines can ever offer" (HII, 143).

A more comedic version of the need to hear and record voices allows for bits of lighter-heartedness in *How It Is*. Earlier fictions multiplied the internal dynamics of narration; this time Beckett siphons off the writing functions into separate named characters, a witness and a scribe. First mentioned in Part I, they grow into the comedy duo of Krim and Kram, brought onstage as Part II begins its preparations to end. Krim sits aloof, writing down some fraction of the words that he hears, as if he's producing the broken packets of narrative that comprise the novel. Kram is cast as a witness by means of a strong lamp that allows him to see in the dark of the mud landscape. He grows into an absurd character who can't wait to be finished with this unpleasant job, but continues for the honor of his ancestral name. These writing figures keep their physical distance from the story they are allegedly inscribing. But they have to be there; the narrator requires acts of witness so as not to lose everything to the mud.

How can such a vision close? As usual in Beckett's prose, the ending is anticipated long before it arrives. The intense desire to be finished (or dead), is always in tension with a deep reluctance to leave life behind. The tension is freely expressed by Beckett's narrators, but it's also acted out by the fluctuations of the long endings, when an impatience to be done is delayed by the sudden introduction of new material or fragmented repeats of old. I find it helpful to imagine Beckett's endings as the last pages of a musical score, when the piece is winding up, but will not end until it has repeated or varied earlier themes, made harmonic announcements of finality, and teased us with one more passage before the final chords are struck.

At the end of *How It Is*, the narrator predictably confesses that there's only been one voice all along. There's nothing left but a solitary being, alone in the mud. No further inventions can distract the narrator from a lonely encounter with the fear of death. Capital letters blare out again, as if carved on his own back, but they receive no response. The last of them spell out it out: "I MAY DIE"; "I SHALL DIE" (HII, 147). And there the writing can come to rest.

"In the last pages," Beckett explained to Donald McWhinnie, "he is obliged to take the onus of it on himself and of the lamentable tale of things it tells" (*Letters*, 3:327). The moralistic overtones surprise me; they suggest an author who feels guilty for having written a book like this. Nevertheless, *How It Is* had served its purpose. Beckett had been trying to force himself to write a prose work in French for nearly a decade, and he berated himself because he wasn't doing it. This tale expresses something of the torture he imposed on himself, to get himself going again in a new work. In both form and content, *How It Is* pushed the horizons of fiction well beyond those of *The Unnamable*, teetering perilously on the edge of recognizable narrative. With that effort behind him, Beckett would never again feel the need to write another prose work of any length. When he returned to *Company* and other prose works during his final decade, the pieces would be short, and composed in brief, readable phrases.

Exhausted after finishing the book, Beckett wrote to Tonny Van Velde in August 1960. "I am as hollow as an old radish. I would like to spend two months in the country digging holes, filling up each one as I go with the earth from the next one" (*Letters*, 3:347). The image harks back to a passage from *The Unnamable*, where the narrator yearns for some physical job to take the place of writing: "some little job with fluids, filling and emptying, always the same vessel, I'd be good at it, it would be a better life than this" (*TU*, 391). Both fantasies wish to annul speech and writing in purposeless labor. Yet they express something essential about the writing life as Beckett may wearily have imagined it. Each new literary form is filled with a reshuffle of situations and obsessions lifted from the last. And each newly prepared hole in the ground is a fresh invitation to repopulate the void.

As if in recoil from *How It Is*, Beckett immediately engrossed himself in a new play, leaving behind the (allegedly) all-male domain of the novel. He planted his heroine Winnie in a mound of earth, where she talks her way through the long days of remaining life as the ground gradually swallows up more and more of her body. Perhaps, in *Happy Days*, he was shoveling the mud from *How It Is* into a new form, one about the simple terror of being buried alive.

Letters to Barbara Bray show him taking pleasure in figuring out how to stage his "imbedded female solo machine" (*Letters*, 3:365). Even though she was visibly present onstage, Winnie required an audience and a witness. He worried about "how to get her to speak without speaking to herself or to the public or to the merely imaginary interlocutor. And yet alone on the stage, riddle me that our Cambridge scholar" (*Letters*, 3:362). At first he invented a barely visible husband for Winnie, wanting that second character to be "as close to a mere ear as possible—and dubious as the divine" (*Letters*, 3:369).

As the play developed in Beckett's hands, that powerful need for a familiar listener would become a major theme of *Happy Days*. Just as *How It Is* required a separate witness and scribe, there had to be someone located inside the work, not just a theater audience or a private reader, to bear witness to the being who struggles to cheer herself onward on in the face of extinction. The wonderful phrase "and dubious as the divine" brushes up against the comforting fantasy of a god that watches over the individual follies of people on earth, or perhaps a great narrator in the sky that records and comments on our inner murmurings as they pass into oblivion. Even amid the cruelty of its relationships, *How It Is* had revealed a Beckett who knows that humans cannot bear to be without others who hear and validate the special truth of their existence.

LOST PERSONS, CHERISHED THINGS

I confuse them, words and tears, my words are my tears, my eyes my mouth.

—Samuel Beckett, *Texts for Nothing*, 8

When he was 70, Beckett received notice from Peggy Beckett, wife of his uncle James, that his cousin Sally Sinclair had died. His immediate response was a near-equivalent of silence.

Thank you for your letter.
Sad news of Sally's death.
I can't grieve for the dead.

Nevertheless, the next sentence recalled another uncle's response on the day of Bill Beckett's death forty-three years earlier, and included a sweet memory of his mother: "I think of Gerald, June 1933, in the porch at Cooldrinagh, to the scent of the verbena mother so loved, saying to her, Well, May, he's got it over. What is it all about, in the end, for us all, from the cry go, but get it over?" (*Letters*, 4:431–2). Beckett's parents may have "got it over," but he had not gotten over them. In a previous letter to his cousin John Beckett, he'd recalled that moment in a starker way: "I can still see

Gerald at that hall door the day father died. 'Well, May, he's got it over'" (Letters, 4:395).

Gerald Beckett, brother of Bill and James Beckett, had been a favorite with his young nephew. Gerald's way of announcing that the last struggle had ended gave homage to the dead for enduring the unwilled burden of life and death. It did not indulge feelings of grief and abandonment in those who had suffered the loss. Beckett would expand his uncle's approach to the point of personal mythology when he persistently linked the moment of birth to the beginning of death. This gesture collapses all the time between, like a wish to get it all over before it even begins. Beckett's narratives flaunt that idea while they act out just the opposite desire: to string time along, so as to extend the life of his characters as long as possible. In the course of writing about Beckett I have come to expect, and respect, this conflict as a central component of his artistic vision. The accordion-like alternation between time stretched and time collapsed feels true, not only to our apprehension of life and death, but to our ordinary experience. "It seems like yesterday," we say of a far-off event, or "It seemed to go on forever."

Beckett's impulse to shy away from direct expressions of grief does not mean he did not feel them. It was in part a reaction against the ostentatious outward rituals of mourning that May Beckett imposed on the household after her husband's death, expressing his distrust of sentimentality. It kept his own grief separate and private, free from the kind of mourning behavior that would be socially recognized and approved. Just as he fought off nostalgia, he fought off the response to loss that directed attention to the bereaved rather than the dead. His lasting sadness was enclosed and protected by his art, which would always be inhabited by memories of his parents. Bill Beckett's long green greatcoat, and his need to walk far and wide in the fields and hills, would be reincarnated over and over. May Beckett's decline and the prolonged period of waiting for her death could be seen as the essential plot of Beckett's postwar dramas and fictions.

Bill Beckett's sudden and fatal heart attacks in June 1933 could hardly have come at a worse time for his 27-year-old younger son. Sam was moored back in Ireland, undergoing operations for a life-long plague, stubborn cysts on his neck and palm. He had no serious job prospects, no clear future. *Dream of Fair to Middling Women* was rejected everywhere. During his hospital recovery he learned that Peggy Sinclair had unexpectedly died of tuberculosis. The next month his father died. Sam's nightly panic attacks returned.[1]

His father had been the central support of his life. The two of them walked for miles in the hills around their Foxrock suburb, often in silence, enjoying each other's company and the escape from May's household requirements. Bill Beckett had privately supported Sam with funds when he was desperate. He had been the founder of his sons' very athletic young lives. Two months before he died, Beckett's love for him came through in a letter to Tom McGreevy:

> Lovely walk this morning with Father, who grows old with a very graceful philosophy. Comparing bees & butterflies to elephants and parrots & speaking of indentures with the leveller. Barging through hedges and over the walls with the help of my shoulder, blaspheming and stopping to rest under colour of admiring the view. I'll never have any one like him.   (*Letters*, 1:154)

A bit uncanny, this letter, as if Beckett already knew he was about to lose his father. Once it had happened, McGreevy was entrusted with a final scene.

He was in his sixty first year, but how much younger he seemed and was. Joking and swearing at the doctors as long as he had breath. He lay in the bed with sweet pea all over his face, making great oaths that when he got better he would never do a stroke of work. He would drive up to the top of Howth and lie in the bracken and fart. His last words were "Fight fight fight" and "what a morning." All the little things come back—mémoire de l'escalier.

I can't write about him. I can only walk the fields and climb the ditches after him.   (*Letters*, 1:165)

After creating so vivid a portrait of his father's last days, why say "I can't write about him"? Perhaps Beckett felt there was something wrong in memorializing Bill as if he were a character in a novel. His mind retreats to the silent walking he had shared with his late companion. Later, the memories would be dissolved into the fictions. I hear echoes of the father's death as late as *Ohio Impromptu* (1981), when the bereaved lover has moved out of the home he had shared with his beloved. The move does not forestall his grief, and the panic attacks that followed for Beckett after Bill Beckett's death revive. "In this extremity his old terror of night laid hold on him again. After so long a lapse as if never been…White nights now again his portion. As when his heart was young."[2]

May Beckett's death in August 1950 was followed all too closely by the death from lung cancer of Sam's older brother Frank in September 1954. In childhood the brothers had been close; both excelled and competed in innumerable sports and chess matches, and Sam had followed Frank from one school to the next. Frank had been the obedient older son who went, rather unwillingly, into his father's business and tended the home front while Sam vanished into another life. Here was another family member he knew he had abandoned. When he heard about Frank's diagnosis at the end of May, Sam went immediately back to Dublin, helping

Frank's wife Jean with nursing and garden work through the three and a half months to the end. Caring for Frank inevitably brought back their parents' deaths, but it was especially excruciating because Jean and Sam were under medical orders not to tell the patient of his condition. The deception enforced on them would have been intolerable for Beckett, who demanded honesty and despised social feints. James Knowlson ends his account of this time with the sentence "The past four months had been among the most traumatic of his life."[3] Frank's death left him, at 48, the sole surviving member of his immediate family.

The published letters from his brother's house in Killiney keep Beckett's professional life going, and mention the ordeal in mostly telegraphic ways. By August he was chafing at the bit: "Here the damnable round continues. Complications are beginning and God knows for what atrociousness we are bound" (*Letters*, 2:493). He was yearning for release, measuring the time he had left, repeatedly warning himself it would go on for at least another two months. To Tonny van Velde, he wrote, "My life here—nothing; better not mentioned. It will end like everything else, and the way again will be free that goes toward the only end that counts" (*Letters*, 2:495). He could not grieve or begin to recover until he could sequester himself for six weeks in Ussy, after his return to France. Trips to Ireland were, by now, all too deeply associated with the mortality of his family.

In the immediate wake of Frank's death, Beckett began writing a new play that would eventually become *Endgame*. Its bitterness captures some of Beckett's reactions to his months of caring for Frank. The dying man Hamm is blinded and coughing up blood, as Frank was hoodwinked about the seriousness of his lung cancer. The caregiver Clov is trying to make the days go by pretending that things are going along according to routine. Trapped by his obligation, he wants only to leave. The parents in their garbage can coffins can't be kept from intruding on the scene, where they do provide the only somewhat affectionate comic relief. What Sam actually felt about his brother after their life paths had diverged is, however, something the play will not tell us. Later, he would become a loving supporter of Frank's son, the flautist Edward Beckett, as his nephew developed his career in music at the Paris Conservatoire. He and Suzanne, herself a graduate of the Conservatoire, helped Edward to loosen the Irish toils that had kept Frank in place.

Beckett's letters of condolence to friends are strangely comforting in their realism and refusal of set formulae. To Tonny van Velde, on the death of her mother in 1952: "It's something I am very familiar with. More familiar every day. Nothing to be done, nothing to be said; nothing but take it, and watch out for sleepless nights" (*Letters*, 2:343). He understands that you don't "get over" grief; it just becomes a more familiar companion. When Tonny's long-depressed partner was dying in 1977, Beckett hoped his life would not be prolonged. "Your sad letter yesterday," he wrote. "My heart goes out to you. I hope that's the end for him. It's scandalous to be making efforts to be bringing him back to his wretchedness. Don't blame yourself. You have been wonderful to him" (*Letters*, 4:478). Her desolation after the loss brought the sympathetic understanding that deepened in those later years: "What can I tell you? You are greatly to be pitied. What you've done for F., no one else would have. That gives meaning to a life. You'll say it's easy for me to talk" (*Letters*, 4:491). It was certainly not easy for Beckett to talk about meaning, but he was right to use the word, as he imagined a possible comfort in the knowledge that Tonny had done everything she could.

When Alan Schneider lost his father in 1963, Beckett's identification with him issued in a voice of wonderful emotional intelligence.

> I know your sorrow and I know that for the likes of us there is no ease for the heart to be had from words or reason and that in the very assurance of sorrow's fading there is more sorrow. So I offer you only my deeply affectionate and compassionate thoughts and wish for you only that the strange thing may never fail you, whatever it is, that gives us the strength to live on and on with our wounds. (*Letters*, 3:582)

By far the starkest and most enigmatic of Beckett's condolence letters is the one he wrote to Barbara Bray in 1958, when she had confided her sorrow after the death of her estranged husband.

> And I have so little light and wisdom in me, when it comes to such disaster, that I can see nothing for us but the old earth turning onward and time feasting on our suffering along with the rest. Somewhere at the heart of the gales of grief (and of love too, I've been told) already they have blown themselves out. I was always grateful for that humiliating consciousness and it was always there I huddled, in the innermost place of human frailty and lowliness. To fly there for me was not to fly far, and I'm not saying this is right for you. (*Letters*, 3:119)

Beckett leaps first to a kind of universalizing distance, akin to Wordsworth's poem about the dead child Lucy, "Rolled round in earth's diurnal course/With rocks and stones and trees."[4] The suffering of grief is a universal condition, but Beckett's "humiliating consciousness" turns its passion into a kind of deception. "Somewhere at the heart of the gales of grief (and of love too, I've been told) already they have blown themselves out." What could that mean? That there's a coldness of heart at the center of strong emotion? That strongly expressed "gales" of emotion are not to be trusted? Is the image of huddling in this humiliation an expression of the guilt associated with loss? Or is it a recognition of the relief at the heart of loss, based on his experiences of waiting for a prolonged dying process to end? I can only glimpse some lifelong disturbance, perhaps a belief that his own failure to love had been responsible for the suffering and death of people close to him.

Twenty years earlier, Beckett had ended a furious rant against his mother in a 1937 letter to Tom McGreevy in this way:

> And if a telegram came now to say she was dead, I would not do the Furies the favour of regarding myself even as indirectly responsible.
> Which I suppose all boils down to saying what a bad son I am. Then Amen. It is a title for me of as little honour as infamy. Like describing a tree as a bad shadow. (*Letters*, 1:553)

The disturbance here is closer to the surface. At that moment he *did* fear he would be somehow responsible for May's death, at the same time that he almost wished for a telegram announcing that end. He accepts the title of "bad son" while refusing it: a substantial tree, or son, should not be known only by a shadow it may cast. As with the obscure "gales of grief" image, I feel I'm in the presence of some deeply unresolved tangle that Beckett cannot, or will not, sort out. In the fiction, it appears in all the passages that bring up the possibility of loving only to obscure it, silence it, or undermine it.

In a calmer vein, Beckett expressed his sense of global sadness in a later note to Barbara Bray. "I don't know why time isn't helping you, it has all my old troubles churned into emulsion till tears are about nothing & everything" (*Letters*, 3:207–8). Tears, the body's involuntary language of sorrow, were preferable to gales of

verbal emotion. Wide-open eyes full of unexplained tears sometimes appear, apparently out of nothing, in the writing. In *Texts for
Nothing* Beckett had nudged at a direct relation between words and
tears. In Text 6 the narrator, distrustful of words, admonishes
himself. "But first stop talking and get on with your weeping, with
eyes wide open that the precious liquid may spill freely, without
burning the lids, or the crystalline humour, I forget, whatever it is
it burns." *Whatever it is it burns* turns the image around, admitting
that grief hurts no matter how wide the eyes are open. Text 8 tries
out a formula: "I confuse them, words and tears, my words are my
tears, my eyes my mouth."[5] *My words are my tears.* I can't think of
any more eloquent description of Beckett's work.

Perhaps the sense of accumulating grief underlies the way
Beckett's characters keep coming back, like revenants. They are
put away at the end of one novel only to show up again in a later
one. The figure of Malone keeps revolving around the Unnamable
even after he bans "all those Murphys, Molloys and Malones."
Belacqua keeps popping up, as late as *How It Is*. Watt does a second
turn in *Mercier and Camier*. These characters won't disappear in
Beckett's mind, nor will the memories of his parents and early
loves. The appearance of new creatures and things within his fictions may be celebrated by his narrators as renewed prompts to go
on writing, but when they fade away they are not much mourned,
lest they show up again later.

I have come to think that Beckett's work expresses alternations
of attachment and abandonment more freely through possessions that come and go than through the deaths or disappearances
of characters. We know that he did not care for accumulating
things, preferring only the most basic amenities in housing and
furnishing. We know about the neatness of his habits, and the

careful way he arranged his books and his array of tools in the shed at Ussy. He liked spareness in the places he lived, as if it offered more room for the work of feeling and writing. Extraneous stuff was just distracting. Along with his lifelong dislike of bourgeois furnishing, Beckett's war experience and his status as a foreigner in France meant that he might be called again to pull up stakes at a moment's notice. But he well knew that when possessions are sparse, each one that's kept gathers a special weight of memory and feeling.

The urge to keep meaningful objects, and then to throw them away, inhabits both Beckett and the creatures he invented. Beckett confessed to Charles Duthuit in 1951 that he couldn't find a certain letter. "I am going to look again. But it may have been the victim of the last fit of Occam's razor as I practice it, when the humour takes me, on anything that is lying around, often to my own disadvantage. Forgive me, dear friend, if it no longer exists" (*Letters*, 2:274). His joke about Occam's razor, the principle that things should not be multiplied unless they are essential, covered his chagrin at being caught in the act of throwing out a friend's letter. His characters also play the game of come and go, attaching themselves to objects that they suddenly toss away or leave behind.

Beckett's protagonists pride themselves when they put found objects to new uses, avoiding the need to multiply things. Molloy likes wrapping himself with the Times Literary Supplement, which he finds especially well adapted to keep him warm under his greatcoat. We learn in *Malone Dies* that Macmann, a character who boasts little physical skill, could exhibit great dexterity when he repaired or replaced the buttons on his greatcoat, or repaired his worn-out boots with willow-bark. He too is given the gift of improvisation and repair, making use of old materials so as not to require new ones. The narrator of *How It Is* finds that a tin-opener can double as a torture device. Beckett also loves to joke about the way things turn up unexpectedly in his narratives. Like props in a play, they appear when they are needed to move the story forward, and Beckett enjoys pointing out the fact that he has planted them there. One funny example, from the story "The End," concerns the fashioning up of a shelter in a small boat. To keep the rats out of this coffin-like space, the narrator makes "a kind of lid with stray boards. It's incredible the number of boards I've come across in my lifetime. I never needed a board but there it was, I had only to stoop and pick it up" (*Stories and Texts for Nothing*, 68). Amazing what fiction can provide for the ingenious!

Keeping track of things as they come and go can be a source of amusement, or bemusement, for Beckett's narrators. Molloy ponders on the shape of a mysterious small metal object he has stolen from Lousse's house after his captivity there. He describes it carefully, intrigued exactly because he can imagine no possible use for it. The affection he develops for it keeps him from selling it. An object without apparent use or effect is a friendly inhabitant of Molloy's world; it evokes wonder. He is also prone to throwing things away in fits of boredom or irritation. He tosses his sixteen sucking stones after they have entertained him long enough with arcane mathematical permutations, in his effort to suck each one in its turn. Attachment and abandonment: in Beckett's world that is the rule, whether he's speaking of other people, objects, or the endurance of life itself.

Things can be carriers of memory and emotion. When Molloy completes his descriptions of A and C, he begins his own story by taking up his crutches and going down the road, where he finds the green bicycle he didn't know he had. The reunion is met with an aria of love, and a happy sequence of bicycle memories follows, until they're reluctantly put away under the imperative to go to his mother. Like involuntary memories, certain objects are cherished because they bring previous selves alive—but only for a time. When he leaves Lousse's house, Molloy leaves his bicycle behind without difficulty. He puts off speaking of his hat or greatcoat; the time to speak of them will be later, when he draws up an inventory of possessions. Such an inventory belongs with the far end of life, when people draw up wills and last testaments. The urge to be finished with it all crops up in the anticipation of making that list, but it has to be postponed in the name of continuing life.

Malone Dies develops questions of possession and inventory more fully, probing the possible meanings of both terms. When does something belong to someone? At what point does ownership begin or cease? How is it that objects can become cherished extensions of the self?

As Malone sets out his initial writing plan, he decides he will do his inventory once he's run out of stories, should that occur before he manages to die. His possessions lie in a heap in the corner of the room he lies in, and he can pull them toward him or send them back to their corner by means of a long hooked stick. The physical connection is already fragile; he can no longer carry them in the pockets that accommodate most of the objects that Beckett's homeless wanderers pick up.

But Malone can't wait for the end to speak of his possessions. Early on he draws them to him to make sure he has them all in mind, so that he'll be sure of them when he draws up his list of "chattels personal. I presume it is an obsession" (MD, 190). Some items that he recalls are not there; some he had forgotten are there instead, but he decides to call them all his. Among them is a little wrapped package that holds some mystery yet to be uncovered. Like the strange object Molloy cherishes, the little packet is valued for some surprise it might still promise. It's a sign of ongoing life.

Despite his resolution to put off the inventory until last, Malone panics again at a later point: "Quick quick my possessions" (MD, 239). He knows he's probably not at the end, but he's overcome with the need to try the inventory anyway. This time his account is based only on memory, and includes a needle ingeniously stuck for safety into two corks, the bowl of a pipe discarded by somebody else and used for storage, and "little portable things in wood or stone" that Malone had picked up and put in his pocket, "often with tears," where he could fondle and love them. They become his companions, which sometimes "gave me the impression that they too needed me." When their term of life is over, they warrant a kind of funeral: "And those of which I wearied, or which were ousted by new loves, I threw away, that is to say I cast round for a place to lay them where they would be at peace for ever" (MD, 241).

It's too easy to dismiss these emotional relationships with objects as symbolic substitutes for the love and loss of people. Beckett implies that they are also relationships of use, comfort, and affection, that help Malone remember what he was and what he is. I find his list of possessions especially endearing because they are so odd and random, completely disconnected from the commercial marketplace or the necessities of living. Whether present to the touch, thrown away, or lost, their keeper develops a special human relationship with each one, and imagines that they respond in kind. His anthropomorphic fantasy suggests a tender capacity to love, so long as it's not associated too closely with loving another particular person. Dwelling on his objects enlarges Malone's imaginative space as his body shuts down. They remind him of earlier experiences when he reached out to the natural world or connected, however distantly, with the lives of others.

With objects as with people in Beckett's world, keeping does not last. As more and more objects from the past keep thronging his mind, Malone becomes uneasy and tries to place limits on the meaning of possession. He decides to call something his own only if he knows where it is and thinks he can lay hold of it. As if on cue, the next section begins with disaster: he can no longer find his stick. Now that the objects are physically inaccessible, they are no longer his. The inventory collapses; he no longer knows what's his and what is not.

Malone's ambivalence about holding onto life makes him increasingly nervous. Is it a blessing in disguise to become dispossessed? He has let go, almost, of the connections afforded by the objects he has lived with. His only possessions are now the implements of writing essential to the record of life that Malone wants to keep. The notebook is humanized; it "is my life, this big child's exercise-book, it has taken me a long time to resign myself to that. And yet I shall not throw it away" (MD, 267). The writing is what's left of his hold on living and on his "life," an autobiographical record on paper. If it lacks the finality of inventory, it is nonetheless full of invention.

Beckett made extensive use of objects again when he came to write the play *Happy Days*. He gives his protagonist a large black shopping bag that contains her props, which are mostly grooming equipment and visual aids: a toothbrush and toothpaste, spectacles, a magnifying glass, a handkerchief, a parasol, a mirror, a hat, a nail file, lipstick. A comb and brush are mysteriously missing; the losses have already begun. The stage business in this play is intricate, as the actress has to co-ordinate her speeches with an ongoing physical dialogue with her objects. Winnie is troubled throughout Act I by her inability to read some advertising slogan on the handle of her toothbrush, even with spectacles or the magnifier, both elaborately cleaned by the handkerchief. The business of getting through daily mundanities is prolonged.

The pathos of Winnie's situation can be overwhelming. Annihilation is visibly coming for her with an added horror, the prospect of burial alive. In the face of it she carries on talking, cheering herself on, putting on her smile, and maintaining a stream of marital coaxing and prodding to keep up some semblance of connection with her monosyllabic husband. Is she painfully silly, a portrait of a ditzy dame who can't shut up or face reality? I think not. Winnie is doing what many people do when confronted with calamity, loss, or death: she goes on operating through lifelong habit. Although Willie is almost hidden and there is no one to look at her, she brushes her teeth, files her nails, applies lipstick, puts on her hat. Her only reading material is the partly illegible advertising slogan on the handle of her toothbrush. These measures help her get through one day, then another. She goes on taking things out of her bag and putting them back in, as people go on using things and putting them back where they belong. She can't do anything about her death sentence, but she attempts to carry on with a sense of personal dignity as long as she can. If some tiny moment of connection occurs with Willie, she will call that a happy day. She dreams of a force stronger than gravity that would pull her up so she could "simply float up into the blue."[6] You might say Winnie is doomed not to give up.

The anomalous object in her bag is the revolver. It appears just when Winnie is telling herself not to rely too much on the distractions offered by her bag.

> Do not overdo the bag, Winnie, make use of it of course, let it help
> you when you…along, when stuck, of course, but cast your mind
> forward, something tells me, cast your mind forward, to the time
> when words must fail—and do not overdo the bag.   (HD, 151)

The ellipsis shows her retreat from saying a word like "despair." As
if in answer, the revolver is brought out of the bag. Winnie rejects
it, though she knows it's there to put her out of her misery when
despair overtakes her. "Oh I suppose it's a comfort to know you
are there," she says to it, "but I'm tired of you" (HD, 151). She refuses
to put it back in the bag, so the gun lies displayed on the mound
for the rest of the play, kept apart from her acknowledged possessions. From one point of view it's Beckett's wry joke about stage
props: this gun will *not* go off in the final act, because by then
Winnie's arms are buried and she can no longer reach it. More
seriously, the question of suicide is placed right in front of the
audience. Beckett had been interested in suicide as an idea since
his youth in Paris, but it remained an idea. When his characters
consider it—as Molloy does when he is propped up in a blind alley
after leaving Lousse's house—they reject it, as Winnie does here.
The instinctual pull of life is always too strong, even in Beckett's
universe of disintegration.

Like her fictional counterparts, Winnie cannot reliably enumer-
ate the contents of her bag. She prefers to think that there may be
hidden treasures or comforts remaining. A musical box does
show up briefly. At the same time, objects begin to disappear. Her
parasol goes up mysteriously in flames. She smashes her mirror
and throws it away. She says that both things will be there again
tomorrow, "to help me through the day" (HD, 154). As they are
stage props in a theater, she is right about that; they will be intact
for the next night's performance.

When Winnie next appears in Act II, the bag is still there, but all of her possessions have, like Malone's, become inaccessible. She can barely see protruding parts of her own face. Sound and memory take the place of things. She tries to console herself with the prospect of autobiography. "There is my story of course, when all else fails" (HD, 163). The effort doesn't go far. The end comes when her husband Willie, "dressed to kill" (!) crawls around the mound and looks at her for the first time in the play, as if he's coming to court her again. He calls her by her pet name, Win. She is ecstatic. The expression she sees in his eyes, however, is horror.

Happy Days was written in the aftermath of another death that saddened Beckett deeply. Ethna MacCarthy, physician and poet, had been a close friend and unrequited love of Beckett's during their undergraduate days at Trinity College Dublin. In 1956 she married another colleague and friend, A.J. (Con) Leventhal, after the death of his first wife. Three years later, in May 1959, she died of cancer. In December 1958 Beckett returned to Dublin to see her for the last time, staying at his late brother's house and visiting the pair daily with helpful aids, as his friend visibly worsened. As he had done after Frank's death, Beckett retreated to Ussy to recover, and began *How It Is. Happy Days*, which followed close on its heels, was the first Beckett work with a female protagonist who was not, like Mrs. Rooney in *All That Fall*, part of an acting ensemble. Was the play a well-concealed tribute to Ethna MacCarthy's endurance of untreatable cancer? I can't answer that question, but Beckett's work was often a response to a personal loss that could only be properly grieved and memorialized in the form of art.

As he and Suzanne grew frailer with age, and close friends began to die, Beckett became more direct in his expressions of grief and consolation. Suzanne turned 80 in 1980; Sam was six years younger, but had always been besieged by physical difficulties. In the late 1970s they began to vacation regularly on the beaches of Morocco, going for a restorative month twice or three times a year. They were there when Con Leventhal died, also of cancer, on October 3, 1979. Leventhal had moved to Paris after his wife's death, and Beckett saw him frequently. When he returned to Paris from Tangiers, Beckett caught up with his correspondence, announcing the death of his friend in stunned phrases. To Jocelyn Herbert in New York: "Sad days here. My old friend Con Leventhal died here of cancer early this month. A friendship of over 50 years through thick and thin. Now ashes in urn nr. 21501, in the basement of Père Lachaise Columbarium" (*Letters*, 4:513). His shocked sense of loss comes through the spaces between the factual notations.

The following month, Beckett began to write one of his most haunting prose works, *Ill Said Ill Seen*. It brings a dead woman back to presence as she endures the last stages of her life. She is placed in a small cabin among fields, near a large tomb, which she visits in all seasons although she is said, in a beautifully balanced sentence, to be nearly immobile: "Such helplessness to move she cannot help."[7] She is, apparently, both mourner and mourned. Who knows what the tomb contains; perhaps Beckett's dead father, perhaps all whom he had lost. When the woman appears in the narrator's inner vision, he describes what he sees or imagines, but, like an involuntary memory, she often disappears from his inner vision only to reappear at long intervals.

> From one moment of the year to the next suddenly no longer there. No longer anywhere to be seen. Nor by the eye of flesh nor by the other. Then suddenly there again. Long after. So on. Any other

would renounce. Avow, no one. Any other than this other. In wait
for her to reappear. In order to resume. Resume the—what is the
word? What the wrong word?   (IS, 51).

The missing word calls attention to the impossible relationship
between the speaker and a ghost: what would it mean to resume,
in such a case? Still, he refuses to renounce his attachment or to
pretend that he's not still haunted by the old woman, who may be
another late-life incarnation of May Beckett. She would be the one
carrying a cross or a wreath to her husband's grave in early spring-
time. The speaker dreads that reminder of her ritualized bereave-
ment, yet lies in wait for her image to return to his inner vision.
Her death and his mourning may be invisible to others, but they
are never finished.

When she is not "there" in his imagination, he turns his attention to objects that survive her, endowing them with the emotional
weight that attaches to things used and cherished over a lifetime.
Tears come when he glimpses her image lifting long skirts to reveal
old-fashioned boots and stockings, or when he sees "the flagstone
before her door that by dint by dint her little weight has grooved.
Tears" (IS, 51). The physical wearing of time in "by dint by dint"
becomes almost audible in its echo of "little by little," and the gradual denting of the flagstone as she repeatedly steps on it.

The "old deal spindlebacked kitchen chair" in which the woman
habitually sat acquires a life of its own (IS, 45). When she is invisible
to the narrator it "exudes its solitude. For want of a fellow-table."
Nearby there is "an antique coffer. In its therefore no lesser solitude."
He returns to the chair. "But this night the chair. Its immovable air.
Less than the—more than the empty seat the bared back is piteous"
(IS, 62). Beckett personifies the chair and the coffer, as if they were
feeling the gusts of lonely mourning that objects left behind can

bring to the bereaved. By coming at it slant, pouring his most expressive sadness into these pathos-ridden objects, he could, I think, bring tears from a stone. The "bared back" of a cheap old spindle chair, like the vulnerable bone structure of an ancient body, captures in a flash the essence of grief and pity.

In an even more astonishing passage Beckett imagines the buttonhook that the woman had used to button her old-fashioned boots. The details of this tiny object, with its long history of damage and repair, are brought to trembling life in the image of a hooked fish:

> Of tarnished silver pisciform it hangs by its hook from a nail. It trembles faintly without cease. As if here without cease the earth faintly quaked. The oval handle is wrought to a semblance of scales. The shank a little bent leads up to the hook the eye so far from dry. A lifetime of hooking has lessened its curvature. To the point at certain moments of its seeming unfit for service. Child's play with pliers to restore it. Was there once a time she did? Careful. Once once in a way. Till she could no more.   (IS, 52)

The narrator lingers on the image to the point of tears, "till suddenly it blurs." "Careful" in both senses of the word, he cannot venture further into the dead woman's past. Some things are beyond restoration, with pliers or with words.

AFTER WORDS

Where, or what, is the endpoint? Of a life, of a piece of writing? How does it cast its light or shadow on what comes before and after? Those are just a few of the many questions Beckett asks. As I grope toward a way of bringing these meditations to a close, I share his desire and reluctance to end. Do I want to make an inventory, get things summed up in paragraphs about places I've been, ideas I've liked, in the course of this narrative? I doubt it. Can I imagine a symphonic ending? Unlike my subject, I don't have the talent for it. Perhaps I can speak of a few things I've found most compelling in my journey with Beckett.

The wonderful and terrible adaptability of human beings. No matter how unbelievable the situation he imagines for them, Beckett's narrator-characters carry on. Given what they're given, they blunder through, as if they were living in reality.

Beckett's poetry of doubt. No one can surpass his ways of bringing to life that chronic churn of mind. No, that last sentence was wrong; that word misses the mark completely. Shall I try making him crawl, or not? You can't hold onto what you think, what you feel, because it will all flow into something else: another mood, another distraction, another obstacle to what can't be called progress.

Beckett's language. So flexible, so aware of its every move, so beautiful in its uncanny rhythms and its brilliantly layered metaphors. No, it can't really be described. Only quoted, in the trust that someone else will hear it too.

The honor he gives to failure, to the helplessness of language. Beckett's penultimate work, *Worstward Ho*, starts by announcing one more raid on the same old impossible task of telling true. "All of old. Nothing else ever. Ever tried. Ever failed. No matter. Try again. Fail again. Fail better."

NOTES

Chapter 1

1. Samuel Beckett, *Three Novels: Molloy, Malone Dies, The Unnamable* (New York: Grove Press, 1958), 31. Further citations in the text.
2. Samuel Beckett, *Watt* (New York: Grove Weidenfeld, 1953), 72. Further citations in the text.
3. Samuel Beckett, *The Complete Dramatic Works* (London: Faber and Faber, 1986), n.p.. Beckett's note precedes *Not I*, 376–83.
4. *The Letters of Samuel Beckett, Vol. 4: 1966–1989*, ed. George Craig, Martha Dow Fehsenfeld, Dan Gunn, and Lois More Overbeck (Cambridge: Cambridge University Press, 2016), 407. Further citations by volume and page in the text.
5. *Beckett, Complete Dramatic Works*, n.p. Beckett's note precedes *That Time*, 388–95.
6. Samuel Beckett, *Proust* (New York: Grove Press, 1970), 27.
7. For example, see Daniel Schacter on memory encoding and retrieval in *Searching for Memory: The Brain, the Mind, and the Past* (New York: Basic Books, 1996).
8. Samuel Beckett, *Company/Ill Seen Ill Said/Worstward Ho/Stirrings Still*, ed. Dirk Van Hulle (London: Faber and Faber 2009), 3.
9. Samuel Beckett, *Stories and Texts for Nothing* (New York: Grove, 1967), 50.
10. Beckett, *Three Novels*, 261–2.
11. Beckett, *Complete Dramatic Works*, 83.
12. Jorge Luis Borges, *Collected Fictions*, trans. Andrew Hurley (New York: Penguin,1998), 324.
13. Beckett, *Complete Dramatic Works*, 435.

Chapter 2

1. *The Divine Comedy of Dante Alighieri, Vol. 2: Purgatorio*, trans. John D. Sinclair (New York: Oxford University Press, 1977), 62–3.

2. *The Letters of Samuel Beckett*, Vol. 1: 1929–1940, ed. Martha Dow Fehsenfeld and Lois More Overbeck (Cambridge: Cambridge University Press, 2009), 205. Further citations by volume and page in the text.

3. Samuel Beckett, *Dream of Fair to Middling Women*, ed. Eoin O'Brien and Edith Fournier (London: Calder Publications, 1993), 12–13. Further citations as *Dream* in the text.

4. *The Letters of Samuel Beckett*, Vol. 2: 1941–1956, ed. George Craig, Martha Dow Fehsenfeld, Dan Gunn, and Lois More Overbeck (Cambridge: Cambridge University Press, 2011), 391. Further citations by volume and page in the text.

5. Samuel Beckett, *More Pricks Than Kicks* (New York: Grove Weidenfeld, 1972), 38.

6. *The Letters of Samuel Beckett*, Vol. 1: 1929–1940, ed. Martha Dow Fehsenfeld and Lois More Overbeck (Cambridge: Cambridge University Press, 2009), 535. Further citations in the text.

7. *The Letters of Samuel Beckett*, Vol. 3: 1957–1965, ed. George Craig, Martha Dow Fehsenfeld, Dan Gunn, and Lois More Overbeck (Cambridge: Cambridge University Press, 2014), 310.

8. James Knowlson, *Damned to Fame: The Life of Samuel Beckett* (New York: Simon and Schuster, 1996), 173. Knowlson offers a rich account of Beckett's therapy.

9. Samuel Beckett, *Murphy* (New York: Grove Press, 1957), 78. Further citations in the text.

Chapter 3

1. Samuel Beckett, *Three Novels: Molloy, Malone Dies, The Unnamable* (New York: Grove Press, 1958), 3–8. Further citations in the text, abbreviated as M, MD, and TU.

2. For an imaginative rendering of Sam and Suzanne during the wartime period, see Jo Baker, *A Country Road, a Tree: A Novel* (New York: Knopf, 2016).

3. Samuel Beckett, *The Complete Dramatic Works* (London: Faber and Faber, 1986), 220.

4. James Knowlson, *Damned to Fame: The Life of Samuel Beckett* (New York: Grove Press, 1996), 319. I am indebted to Knowlson for information in the biographical paragraphs of this chapter.

5. Knowlson, *Damned to Fame*, 317.

6. Samuel Beckett, *Stories and Texts for Nothing* (New York: Grove Press, 1967), 47.

7. *The Letters of Samuel Beckett, Vol. 2: 1941–1956*, ed. George Craig, Martha Dow Fehsenfeld, Dan Gunn, and Lois More Overbeck (Cambridge: Cambridge University Press, 2011), 41. Further citations by volume and page in the text.
8. The story itself would not appear in its entirety until 1955, when it came out as "La Fin" ("The End") in *Stories and Texts for Nothing*.
9. Samuel Beckett, *Mercier and Camier* (New York: Grove Press, 1970), 1. 1.
10. Quoted in Knowlson, *Damned to Fame*, 346.
11. I will return to the inventory theme in Chapter 5.

Chapter 4

1. *The Letters of Samuel Beckett, Vol. 3: 1957–1965*, ed. George Craig, Martha Dow Fehsenfeld, Dan Gunn, and Lois More Overbeck (Cambridge: Cambridge University Press, 2014), 177. Further citations from this volume in the text.
2. See James Knowlson, *Damned to Fame*, 440–2.
3. Samuel Beckett, *How It Is* (New York: Grove Press, 1964), 7. Further citations as HII in the text.
4. Samuel Beckett, *Stories and Texts for Nothing* (New York: Grove Press, 1967), 54–5.

Chapter 5

1. For an account of this period, see Knowlson, *Damned to Fame*, 161–7.
2. Samuel Beckett, *The Complete Dramatic Works*, 446.
3. Knowlson, *Damned to Fame*, 363. I am indebted to his full account of Frank's death.
4. William Wordsworth, "A slumber did my spirit seal." In *William Wordsworth: The Major Works* (Oxford University Press, 1984), 147.
5. Samuel Beckett, *Stories and Texts for Nothing* (New York: Grove, 1967), 105, 111. 111. Further citations as STN in the text.
6. Samuel Beckett, *The Complete Dramatic Works* (London: Faber and Faber, 2006), 151. Further citations as HD in the text.
7. Samuel Beckett, *Ill Said Ill Seen* in *Company etc*, ed. Dirk Van Hulle (London: Faber and Faber 2009), 45. Further citations as IS in the text.

FURTHER READING

H. Porter Abbott, *Beckett Writing Beckett: The Author in the Autograph*. Ithaca, NY: Cornell University Press, 1996.

Jo Baker, *A Country Road, A Tree: A Novel*. New York: Knopf, 2016.

Anthony Cronin, *Samuel Beckett: The Last Modernist*. New York: Da Capo Press, 1999.

Dan Gunn, "Beckett's Letters: The Edition and the Corpus." In *The New Samuel Beckett Studies*, ed. Jean-Michel Rabaté. Cambridge: Cambridge University Press, 2019, 48–64.

Jacob Hovind, "Samuel Beckett's Invention of Nothing: Molloy, Literary History, and a Beckettian Theory of Character." *Partial Answers*, 16.1 (2018): 65–87.

James Knowlson, *Damned to Fame: The Life of Samuel Beckett*. New York: Grove Press, 1996.

INDEX

For the benefit of digital users, indexed terms that span two pages (e.g., 52–53) may, on occasion, appear on only one of those pages.